Transparent

Seeing Through the Legacy of Adoption

by

Gary Coles

MERMERUS BOOKS
AUSTRALIA   2005

The author can be contacted via

booksurge.com.au

First published in 2005

ISBN 1-921019-13-1

Library of Congress Control Number 2005908234

What others have said about the first book by Gary Coles, *Ever After: Fathers and the Impact of Adoption* –

This book ... dispels the myth that all fathers who lose children to adoption don't care about their partners or their children. It shows where the dynamics of fathers are similar to those of mothers, and where there are differences ... Given the paucity of literature on fathers' experiences, this is a seminal resource for all those interested in understanding the impact of adoption on fathers.

Sandra Falconer Pace, 'Canadian Council of Natural Mothers'

Your book pleased and impressed me. I think your work will go a long way towards increasing community awareness about adoption issues from the birth fathers' perspective.

Mercurio Cicchini, author of DEVELOPMENT OF RESPONSIBILITY: THE EXPERIENCE OF BIRTH FATHERS IN ADOPTION

Gary Coles' book wears his heart on its sleeve ... Coles' account is both one of an inward and outward journey. An inward journey of discovery towards what it means to be a birth father some thirty-five years later and an outward quest to find his son. Along the way Coles takes time to develop some themes that appear in the birth mother literature and makes pointers of how our understanding of birth fathers can be advanced.

Gary Clapton, author of BIRTH FATHERS AND THEIR ADOPTION EXPERIENCES

Highly recommended to all affected by adoption, no matter where you' sit' in the triad, I promise you will be touched and enriched by this superbly written book.

Julia Cantrell, editor of 'issues', New Zealand

Ever After *is a book with many layers: a bravely told personal narrative, a call to action for birth fathers and a personal message to Gary Coles' son who has refused so far to meet his birth parents in person.*

Jennifer Speirs, in 'Rostrum, The Voice of Social Work in Scotland'

Having read **Ever After: Fathers and the Impact of Adoption***, I have to say that if there were a tertiary course in 'Adoption Process and Related Trauma', this book would be the guiding text ... I personally have gained so much and it has been a relief to know there are other men out there feeling the same as I have for many years. Thank you Gary for your courage and honesty.*

John Morrison (a birth father) in 'ARMS Update', Western Australia

At last a book about birth fathers written by a birth father! In **Ever After: Fathers and the Impact of Adoption***, Gary Coles has written an honest, articulate account of the experience of surrender and adoption from a perspective rarely presented.*

Nancy Verrier, author of THE PRIMAL WOUND and COMING HOME TO SELF

Dedication

This book is for my three children

You have each enriched my life beyond measure

> *"Grief fills the room up of my absent child"*
> *— William Shakespeare*

Awakenings

"Your life is the fruit of your own doing" – Joseph Campbell

"The bitterest tears shed over graves are for words left unsaid and deeds left undone" – Thomas Carlyle

"My personal trials have taught me the value of unmerited suffering. As my sufferings mounted, I soon realised that there are two ways that I could respond to my situation: either to react with bitterness or seek to transform the suffering into a creative force" – Martin Luther King

"In the middle of difficulty lies opportunity" – Albert Einstein

"Risk! Risk anything! Care no more for the opinions of others, for those voices. Do the hardest thing on earth for you. Act for yourself. Face the truth" – Katherine Mansfield

"... triumph belongs to those who will dare,
To dream and take action, to risk and to share" – Michael Harrison (1997, p70)

CONTENTS

Section Four: Separation and Integration

Section Five: To Spread Our Wings

References

Much Ado About Adoption

Introduction
to the adoption essays

"No legacy is so rich as honesty" — *William Shakespeare*

I am a man with an adoption experience. I have a son who has, since his birth, lived with another family.

My first book, published in 2004, is about the experiences of my fellow birth fathers and me. It is informed by two aspects, the personal and research, which culminate in my advocacy for change – in particular, that birth fathers become more visible. Since the release of *Ever After: Fathers and the Impact of Adoption*, many people have made contact to tell me that I have made a significant contribution to their understanding of what birth fathers think and feel. Some have said that what I wrote has made a difference to their lives.

In October 2004, I toured New Zealand to present seminars based on the contents of the book. The audiences listened attentively and respectfully. Several birth mothers, emphasising that sometimes birth fathers are poorly regarded, told me that I was brave to speak about my experience and findings in public. Whilst I appreciate this compliment, I believe that disclosure is the appropriate response to being a birth father. The seminar attendees, comprising predominantly birth mothers and those in the helping professions, asked numerous questions and said that they appreciated hearing from and learning about birth fathers. In 2005, when these seminars were presented in Australia, the audience responses were similar.

In November 2004, I visited the United States, to attend the Concerned United Birthparents' Retreat. After my presentation, many birth mothers and adopted persons thanked me for encouraging them to consider the inclusion of birth fathers in reunions and their healing.

Whilst I still have not met the son who was separated from me by adoption, I have maintained my journey. My second book addresses what I have discovered for and about myself. Alongside my personal experience, I explore the repercussions of the social practice we call adoption.

Transparent: Seeing Through the Legacy of Adoption expands on some of the material presented in the first book. It also raises and covers fresh subjects, many of which incorporate, but are by no means the sole preserve of birth fathers. With *Ever After: Fathers and the Impact of Adoption*, my primary objective was to inform readers about how birth fathers are affected by adoption. (Previously, whilst much had been written about the impact of an adoption on birth mothers and adopted persons, typically the father was treated as a peripheral, unimportant figure.) In my second book, I bring the birth father into the mainstream, as a member of the family separated by an adoption. Acknowledging birth fathers to this extent is a first in the literature about post-adoption matters.

In the penultimate chapter of my first book, I wrote: "No one who has an adoption experience emerges unscathed. It is the degree to which each person admits to and addresses the impact of adoption on their life that makes the difference" (p227). With *Transparent: Seeing Through the Legacy of Adoption*, my aims are straightforward: to increase an awareness of the repercussions of an adoption for all three members of the family of origin – the birth mother, the birth father and the adopted person, and to assist them to heal their wounds. Whilst I acknowledge the importance of the parents who raise adopted children, adoptive families are not the nucleus of my book.

I believe that what I have to say in *Transparent: Seeing Through the Legacy of Adoption* will be of interest to all persons with adoption experiences, as well as those who know people who are affected by an adoption and the professionals who work for adoption placement and post-adoption support organisations. I hope that my book will encourage workers in the helping professions and those contemplating adoption to consider the alternative of striving to preserve the family of origin.

Transparent is, I believe, a perfect title for a book about adoption. It has the obvious connotations of openness and freedom from deceit, as well as another that uses the meaning of 'across' for the prefix 'trans-', which, when attached to 'parent', etymologically could represent the legal reassignment of a child from one set of parents to another. The sub-title, ***Seeing Through the Legacy of Adoption***, reinforces the aspect of candidness inferred by the title and suggests more. 'Seeing through' indicates drawing upon personal resources, including wisdom and insight, to expose the sham and find the nub. The phrase also embraces a determination and a doggedness to pursue a goal, in this case confronting and addressing the outcomes of an adoption. Overall, 'seeing through' embodies a personal commitment to finding answers through penetrating and persistent probing. The full title emphasises the book's overall theme, that in matters concerning adoption, there is a high value to be placed on candour, or, to put it another way, the importance of being honest with oneself and with others. My emphasis is on the choices that individuals have the capacity to make. Some people with adoption experiences decide to stay within their cocoon. Others opt to emerge and to explore – these are the persons whom my book celebrates.

As an accompaniment to the pre-eminent personal matters, I refer to legislatively condoned impediments and deceptions. Also, I discuss the misrepresentation that can occur in the public portrayal of adoption.

Between the publication of my first and second books, my fundamental position on adoption has not changed. I still believe that there are more humane alternatives. Nothing I see in present adoption practices, particularly intercountry placements, causes me to modify my view. Rather, the separation of the adopted child from not only their birth parents, but a cultural, ethnic and social history, in some instances involving the exchange of substantial sums of money, reinforces my opposition to adoption.

I have chosen the essay format, because it allows me to address a wide range of topics, albeit linked to the fundamental issue of the effects of adoption. An essay is not only 'a composition on a particular topic', but also has the obsolete meaning of 'an experiment or a trial'. The dual meanings are perfect for my purposes, for I believe that adoption is a process, established with good intentions, but beset by tribulations.

This book is in five parts. Section One, *Being There*, is a record, via a series of articles, of my journey. It starts with a background piece, then highlighting specific elements of my progress, builds a picture of my adoption experience. I discuss the advances and the pauses, to much of which, I believe, others may relate. *Pain and Prejudice* (Section Two) contains essays that investigate both the public view of the effects of adoption and an insider's view looking out. The middle section, *Cut to the Core* draws upon previous studies. It focuses on the past and the present and highlights the issues that plague the aftermath of an adoption. Specific personal and interpersonal barriers centred upon deceit, secrecy and denial, which impede the understanding of the outcomes of an adoption, are identified and discussed. Here also, issues specific to birth fathers are addressed. Section Four, *Separation and Integration* is a cause and effect investigation of the emotional wounds inflicted on all three members of the family of origin, caused by their breakup. However, by acknowledging the hurt and embracing honesty, openness and generosity, family members can heal. This part of the book advocates and shows the benefits of including birth fathers in the recovery process, a matter not previously addressed, beyond suggestion, in adoption literature. The final section, *To Spread Our Wings*, is devoted to the future, one in which frankness prevails, both in public communications and within relationships. In particular, it highlights, through a willingness to accept personal responsibility, the capacity of those affected by an adoption to overcome the personal and interpersonal issues that can impede growth.

The majority of the content of ***Transparent: Seeing Through the Legacy of Adoption*** has not been published before. A few of the articles in Section One and Section Two have appeared previously, courtesy of editors, in newsletters published by post-adoption support organisations in Australia and New Zealand. Because their circulation is restricted and local requests to reprint the articles are frequent, I have concluded that the individual pieces might be of interest and value to a wider audience, one that can be reached by a book. An additional benefit of publishing such material in book form is that it is consolidated, not scattered. It represents a body of work.

Because they are common in the literature on adoption, I have chosen to use the terms adopted persons, birth parents and adoptive parents. Where, for example, 'birthmother' is used as a single word in a reference or the original author prefers 'natural mother' or 'adoptee', I have remained faithful to the source. In quotations, I have replicated the original spelling of common words.

I hope that, for those of you who have discovered the benefits of being transparent about your adoption experience, my book is a reinforcement of your actions and the results you have achieved. I hope that, for those people who are on the cusp of exploring the influence of adoption on their lives, including the prospect of reunion, my book provides the catalyst for you to begin your journey of self-discovery and integration. Based on my experience, the journey is absolutely worthwhile.

Transparent

SECTION ONE

Being There

"Being entirely honest with oneself is a good exercise" — *Sigmund Freud*

The opening section of the book tells my story via a series of articles written and in the case of four, first aired between 2001 and 2004. I establish a foundation and then supply the essential elements of my experience, complete with highlights, setbacks, lessons learned, cautionary notes and pointers for others. There are two specific topics that I have addressed in some detail. **Being There** *captures components of my adoption separation and integration story and the resultant personal growth. This segment culminates with some reflections upon my journey.*

This is a truncated version of my adoption narrative. It is taken from a booklet Understanding Birth Fathers, *which I wrote in 2002. The full version of my story appears as Section One of* Ever After: Fathers and the Impact of Adoption. *The summary below sets the scene for the seven articles that follow.*

1. As it happened

I am a birth father. I have been so since 1967, the year my first son was born. His mother and I planned to marry after we finished university in New Zealand, so when Kay became pregnant, the fruit of our love created a predicament. Denied the support of our parents, I panicked and chose not to stand by Kay. I was scared and not equipped at twenty to assume awesome adult responsibilities. Alone, Kay took the only option available to her. She deferred her studies and 'disappeared' to a remote small town to await the birth of a son, who was placed for adoption.

I, as suggested by my parents, put the career threatening 'unfortunate incident' behind me (or so I thought) and got on with 'the rest of my life'. I graduated, found employment as an exploration geologist in Australia, married, and fathered two legitimate children.

However, my career did not blossom. I felt inadequate as a husband and father. I suppressed my feelings, apart from flashes of self-directed anger. My life remained on hold until my first born son turned 21 in 1988. I experienced a profound sense of relief that he had reached his majority; I was no longer responsible for him. Of course, the reality was that I had relinquished the right to be considered his carer before he was born. Here was my guilt surfacing. I was coming out of denial. A nagging ache became a persistent pain, until four years later, I knew for the sake of my well-being that I needed to confront the past. Whilst I was apprehensive about what I might discover, anything seemed better than the status quo. Because I had never known my son and because Kay was the person I had let down, I decided I needed first to make my peace with her. I discovered her married name and home address, wrote a letter and then visited her in New Zealand. She forgave me for my actions more than two decades earlier, a reaction I found overwhelming. We talked about our son and wondered where and, in particular, how he was.

Kay made immediate inquiries. Within two days we knew the names his adoptive parents had given him, but not his surname. It took me some time to digest the fact that my son was a living person and to summon the courage to contact him. First though, I had to declare, twenty-seven years late, the undeniable truth. I requested that my name be added retrospectively, as the father, to my son's original birth certificate. This also was a very significant moment for Kay.

When, however, in collaboration with Kay, I tried to make contact with my son, I discovered that he was not ready to meet either of his birth parents. Profoundly disappointed by his response, I sought, using publicly accessible records, his full name and address. In 2001, I decided to begin sending my son birthday and Christmas cards to show that, in the absence of sanctioned contact, I care about him. I remain hopeful that my son will want to know his birth father.

I wrote this article because I wanted to record the important moments of my journey, from the beginning of my search until the original veto placed by my son expired in 2004. Whilst these are personal highlights, I believe that others may be able to relate to and draw encouragement from my milestones. This article adds to the outline in As it happened, *particularly the post-contact phases. It has not been published previously. James is the adoptive name of my son.*

2. The ninth milestone

The path I have taken on the search for my New Zealand-born son and myself has been attended by milestones. In the thirteen years to date, there have been eight vital events, interspersed with many moments of lesser import.

My first step was, in retrospect, the boldest, because it involved a major personal attitudinal shift. For more than two decades, I had denied that the loss of the family embracing my first born son and his birth mother had left a legacy. As I confronted my buried feelings, what I unearthed caused me trepidation. When I lost my first family, part of me had gone with them – could I recover from the diminution of self-belief and personal virtue that had accompanied this dramatic event? How could I share my secret with the two children of my subsequent marriage? If I was to approach my son and his birth mother, both, I thought likely to be in New Zealand, then surely, after leaving them in the lurch all that time ago, I was liable to be confronted by their disappointment and anger. But remaining cocooned and static seemed the worse option and anathema to my view that life is a journey. Perhaps, despite the reaction I anticipated, my re-appearance could help mother and son to address issues they might have as a result of the adoption.

I reasoned that I should begin my search by locating Kay, the birth mother. She was the person I had failed, leaving her with no alternative, in the social climate of the times, but to relinquish our child to unknown adoptive parents. I visited an office holding public records and discovered her current surname and whereabouts. This was an epiphanous moment. I remember feeling an enormous burden being lifted from my shoulders, of almost fainting with relief from the knowledge that Kay was alive and that I could apologise to her.

The second search milestone occurred as a consequence of the first. After writing to Kay and receiving a letter in return, I visited her, unannounced, to say 'sorry' in person. This was a remarkable event for both of us. A few snatched, interrupted hours were inadequate to talk about everything that had passed since we had last seen each other, a quarter of a century earlier, but we made significant progress. To my great relief, Kay said she bore no grudges against me. Of course, we discussed our son and pondered how life may have treated him.

The next landmark took a little longer to achieve than the second had done. After my visit, Kay had sought non-identifying information about our son from official records and had sent this on to me. As a consequence of being absent at his birth, I was not registered as my son's father. Being forgiven by Kay and seeing information about my son provided the twin triggers for me to contemplate righting this falsehood. Belatedly, I decided to acknowledge my paternity. I filled out the relevant forms, and via Kay, sent them to the appropriate authority. Kay told me that my action was a breakthrough for her, too.

The fourth watershed represented one of the darkest moments of my search. When Kay, via official channels, sought our son's willingness to release identifying information about himself, he responded by placing a veto prohibiting approaches via the relevant government department for ten years. I was included in the veto, which our son could renew in 2004. Both Kay and I were devastated. We could not comprehend why our son appeared to feel threatened by our reaching out to him, especially as the approach had been made through a mediator. (Kay had asked that enquiries be made on behalf of us both, because the registration of my paternity had not yet been processed.)

After this setback, the next milestone took more than three years to achieve. I sought professional advice about the purpose of the veto and, based on the experiences of others, why my son may have placed it. Through publicly available records, I discovered the adoptive name of my son and other identifying information. In my eyes, this made him a real person. Concurrently, I also began to have what I thought were reasonable doubts about whether he had placed the veto himself. The cocktail of information and feelings fomented within me. I reached such an emotional state, that, after agonising about how James might react to my approach and seeking expert reassurances that I was not breaching the conditions of the veto, I decided to telephone my son. He did confirm that, initially, the veto had been placed on his behalf. More significantly, he stated that he was not interested in his birth parents and wanted nothing to do with either Kay or me. The only 'bright' moments in this very awkward conversation were his acknowledgment that he could tell that I cared about him, as well as a reluctant agreement to exchange photographs. These duly arrived three months later. They are amongst the most treasured items in my home.

Again, there was a significant hiatus, before I attained the next stage. James did not want to engage in dialogues with his birth parents, so there seemed to be little point in undermining his now very clear wishes. One personal matter that remained unresolved was my son's original birth certificate. Once I had acknowledged my paternity, I believed that it was my right to see my name recorded on this official document. Under New Zealand law, it seemed that, at face value, I could not access this certificate, unlike, for example, New South Wales, Australia. With the assistance of a fellow birth father, I presented a case that I be granted access to the original birth certificate, which had had my name added as the birth father. My submission was accepted by the court and I was sent a copy of my son's original birth certificate with the names of both his birth parents recorded. When I opened the envelope, I wept with joy. Later, I felt proud, because I was the first birth parent to succeed in New Zealand with such an approach, opening the way for others to follow.

I achieved the seventh landmark within months of the sixth. For some time I had contemplated reinforcing the positive point that James had made when I contacted him by telephone. To show that I continued to care about him, I decided, starting on his 34th birthday in 2001, to send him birthday and Christmas cards. I made it clear in an introductory letter that he need not feel any obligation to reciprocate in kind. To date, my cards appear to have been accepted, in the sense that they have not come back to me labelled 'Return to Sender'. I interpret this as a positive sign.

The eighth significant moment coincided with the publication of my first book, *Ever After: Fathers and the Impact of Adoption*. The veto placed by my son expired in mid-March 2004. Thankfully, he chose not to renew it, perhaps an acknowledgment of my sending greetings to him for the previous three years. I was hopeful that the non-renewal could herald a change in attitude by my son. Later in 2004, I wrote to tell him of my book and a planned promotional tour of New Zealand. I took this initiative as a courtesy to James, so that he would not be surprised by any attendant publicity. I did not receive a reply.

Whilst I have gained enormously from the steps I have taken to date, there remains the ninth milestone – meeting my son. By sending James birthday and Christmas cards, I will continue to issue a subtle invitation for him to join me in reunion. When it does occur, it is probable that our reunion will be both the zenith of my search for my self and my son and the launching of a fresh phase of the journey of discovery.

This succinct piece is a reflection. It underlines the benefits of dialogue between Kay and me, initiated when we met again in 1992. Of course, this discussion would not have taken place but for the actual choices made in 1966–67! Like the movie Sliding Doors, *what follows exposes what might have been, had other paths been taken. I have used this particular style to emphasise the 'what if' elements, absent from other aspects of my narrative.*

3. A family that was not to be

A long time ago, several decades past,
A teenager in a family,
Where sex was never to be raised.
Naive, uncertain, the time of the Vietnam War.
Still seeking an identity,
Looking for love and love looking for me.

Serendipity – finding and sharing love
With Kay; profound, passionate, compassionate.
A life together – forever – the dream,
The plan, but first, studies to complete
Before two will become one,
My first love and me.

Both twenty, powerful feelings ... carried away,
And so a child to come before time.
Plans brought forward, but hurdles to cross.
What will they say, our parents and all?

Transparent

Too young, I am scared and I withdraw my support.
Agony for Kay – plans made alone: go away from home.
A hasty decision taken and a love forsaken,
I leave her grieving for a commitment undone.

I am ashamed; we share letters and I wait
For news of a baby born in a remote rural place.
Separated from his mother distraught,
An infant boy is adopted, to be raised by another family.

A tangled web of emotions, yet still a chance,
But one not taken after the birth.
Kay has forgiven me, but I cannot see
Through my guilt and my stubbornness
That inside her pain and her sorrow
Lies love, still burning and yearning.

And so the critical moment passes,
The opportunities gone then; discussed decades later.
Could we have made it, as a couple or a family
Before or after the birth of our son?

Through the lens of maturity we can see
Marriage had been possible, a young family intact,
Parental shock and disapproval overcome
With unearthed courage and the mending of time.

Reclaiming the relationship less known,
Because of the spectre of a child lost.
Our pain to cloud a life together,
A wondering – why and how is he?
Difficult questions later from him and his kin;
A challenge for the deepest of loves.

Transparent

So, a love found and lost, but never forgotten.
Separate marriages and parallel lives;
Each blessed by wonderful children,
But with regret buried deep
For bonds created and broken
And our family that was not to be.

May our son know and accept the love
We joyfully gave to begin his life.
May his journey be blessed with wisdom
And growth and the certainty of knowing
That behind the sadness and the pain
Of separation are two special people
Willing to help with the healing
Of a family that was not to be.

The no curiosity shock was published in the ARCS Newsletter *of December 2002 and subsequently reprinted in* Branching Out *(March 2003). It was fuelled by my dismay that my son was not interested in his heritage and declined to meet me. I believe that my frustration and disappointment are obvious in this article.*

4. The no curiosity shock

When I reached out to my then 29-year-old son in 1997, he wrote back to tell me that he had thought little about his adoption, and had no interest in his background or further contact. I found his reply daunting. How in the Dickens could he not want to know his birth mother or me, the two persons who gave him life? Are we not part of his identity?

I do know that my son has travelled extensively overseas, which suggests that he is inquisitive about foreign places and cultures. So his curiosity seems to be selective, but definitely turned off in relation to his heritage. Why, I wonder? Because, out of respect for my son's wishes, I am not in a position to ask him for the answers to these burning questions, I have sought clues from the experiences of others.

The authors of the book *Adoption New Zealand: The never-ending story* have this to say: "Most of the adopted people who told us their stories spoke of a deep need to know about their birth families – to meet someone who looks like them and shares their inherited mannerisms, personality traits and interests" (Gillard-Glass and England, 2002, p81). In the same reference, adoptive parent Julie observes that "[my son] is curious about his origins, which seems to me to be the natural way for an adopted person to be" (pp150–151). It is unwise to conclude that these statements apply to all adopted persons, because the sample is biased in favour of those who are prepared to be open about the influence of adoption on their lives.

Many professionals who have studied the impact of adoption hold the view that curiosity about one's origins is both healthy and natural. John Triseliotis, quoted in Keith Griffith's *The Right To Know Who You Are*, told attendees at the Second Australian Adoption Conference in 1978 that "Curiosity about origins and first parentage is something that all adopted people carry with them through life. It is normal ..." (1991, Section 11, p19). I believe that there is a caveat to the first statement – having curiosity is one thing, personally acknowledging it is another. In *The Adoption Triangle*, Robert Jay Lifton builds on Triseliotis' comment about normality. "I think it is the most natural and desirable aspect of any adolescent or adult young person to have curiosity about his forebears, about his biological heritage and the sequence of his generational connectedness. I would consider this the most normal, indeed desirable kind of curiosity ..." (Sorosky, Baran and Pannor, 1989, p137).

That some adopted persons do not choose this path is explored by David Brodzinsky. In the 1993 book *Being Adopted: The Lifelong Search for Self*, he and his co-authors investigate identity development as it applies to adopted persons. They draw the distinction between those who have explored various values and ideologies, then made a commitment to a particular identity and those who have assumed an identity to please others. They term the first state 'identity achievement'. These adopted persons tend to be those whose adoptive families have encouraged open discussion about adoption. Those adopted persons comprising the second category, termed 'identity foreclosure', have often taken on their adoptive parents' attitudes towards adoption, deny that adoption has affected them and claim to have no curiosity about their origins (Brodzinsky, Schechter and Henig, pp102–108). According to Betty Jean Lifton in *Lost & Found: The Adoption Experience*, "When you stifle curiosity about yourself, you stifle many other things as well. You shrink your area of perception. You live in a smaller space" (1988, p53).

David Brodzinsky explores further the role of adoptive parents. He writes: "By creating a family environment characterized by *open, honest and non-defensive communication about adoption issues,* parents not only provide their children with the opportunity and freedom to explore their feelings about the birth parents, and perhaps to form an emotional connection to them, but they also affirm the normality of the process ... This task often challenges adoptive parents, either because of a lack of information about the child's background or because the information available is difficult to deal with and/or violates the parents' value system. Although there are no easy answers for adoptive parents in these circumstances, it is extremely important to emphasize the necessity of helping children feel positive, or at least comfortable with their origins" (Brodzinsky, 2001, pp23–24) [emphasis in the reference].

These views reinforce those expressed by David Kirk in his book *Shared Fate* (1984). Kirk noticed there are essentially two types of adoptive families – those who believe they are identical in every way to biological families and those that have accepted and honoured differences between their own and biological families. In 'acknowledgment of differences' families, the adoptive parents are more likely to create an environment that helps assuage any fears and guilt an adopted person may have about searching for their origins. By contrast, the 'rejection of differences' adoptive parents, who try to downplay adoption issues, convey the message that the subject must be kept under wraps. Adopted persons subjected to this family environment are more likely to repress their curiosity.

An adopted person's response to the degree to which adoption is discussed within their family may be influenced by the persona they have created for themselves to minimise the risk of being abandoned again. Those who assume a compliant false self may have difficulties acknowledging their innate curiosity in a 'rejection of differences' adoptive family, whereas an acting-out adopted person could possibly take the opportunity to rebel against their adoptive parents' wishes that discussion about adoption issues be suppressed.

About the ramifications of, and responses to the adoptive family environment, Evelyn Robinson comments: "Adopted people who deny and reject their natural families ... are actually denying and rejecting themselves. When they acknowledge and embrace their origins, however, they are accepting themselves as whole people, made up of two families, the family into which they were born and the family within which they were raised. Similarly, adoptive parents who deny and reject the natural families of their adopted children are actually denying and rejecting their adopted children" (2000b, p148).

The views expressed above by respected writers do not salve my concerns. Whilst I do not know how my son was raised, I do hope that his curiosity about his origins is dormant, not extinct. I remain optimistic that, in common with some adopted people, a life-changing event such as the birth of children or the death of his adoptive mother may cause James to review his stance. In the meantime, I will continue to send my son birthday and Christmas cards to remind him that I care. My action could make a difference.

Afterthoughts

When I reread this article, it strikes me that some readers may consider my bafflement to be a selfish response, perhaps focussed on meeting my needs, with little regard for my son. However, because I have yet to meet my son, I contend that it would be negligent of me to project what may be happening in his life; in particular why he said he has no interest in his adoption or his birth parents. I believe it is natural that I reflect on the learned views of others, whilst taking care to resist the temptation to draw personal connections.

I acknowledge that James has, as do we all, the right to exercise choice. In his case, he has chosen not to know his antecedents. I cannot change his viewpoint; any reconsideration of his stance is his to make. I realise that in some cases, adopted people prefer to remain detached from their birth parents.

I respect James's current position. I will continue to offer him the opportunity to participate in reunion. I hope that he re-evaluates how he feels about his birth family. Always, James has the capacity to consider the options and make his own decisions.

In contemplating the tone of *The no curiosity shock*, I believe that there is another pertinent factor, which is related to perspective. Most personal narratives about post-adoption experiences are written retrospectively, by participants who have achieved reunion. It is rare for post-adoption stories to be recounted, as I have done, from the stance of a person who is still engaged in the search and contact phases, *ie* is pre-reunion. Birth parents and their adopted children who have met and taken the opportunity to discuss issues of common concern have progressed beyond the stage of wanting to meet. For people who search for their birth relatives, I believe it is natural that their focus be on the desire to achieve reunion. This wish may be accompanied by a longing to make up for lost time – for a birth mother, to know the person who as an infant she perhaps held fleetingly, or in the case of most birth fathers, have never known. Frustrations may be expressed about hurdles encountered, such as a veto or an unwillingness by the other to respond to outreach. Remember, also, that the searcher does not have the luxury, as do those who have accomplished reunion, of knowing the other person, of being in a position to discern the other's readiness to participate, benefit from their viewpoint and, in many cases, incorporate the other's perspective into their narrative. An account written post-reunion may seem to be more considerate and inclusive. In the case of the writer as the searcher, his journey, without the involvement of the person for whom he is searching is, of necessity, one of conjecture, personal discovery and self-healing. Mutual understanding and interpersonal healing are possible only after reunion.

The general topic of access to identifying information is one that has occupied many authors. In my first book I devote an entire chapter, called The right to information, *to this matter. The subject is a central theme of books by Griffith* (The Right To Know Who You Are, *1991) and Sorosky et al* (The Adoption Triangle, *1989, subtitled* Sealed or Opened Records: How They Affect Adoptees, Birth Parents, and Adoptive Parents). *Despite the efforts of these powerful advocates in the fourth quarter of last century, in most countries little progress has been made to allow both adopted persons and birth parents access to information about the adoption and to other members of their birth family. This statement pertains particularly to the United Kingdom and North America.*

In the essay that follows, I concentrate on but one hindrance, the veto. Like The no curiosity shock, My vote on the veto *(published in* issues *in 2002, ie two years prior to the expiry of the veto placed by my son) echoes a personal frustration, against a legal barrier that can hamper the healing of people who have been separated by an adoption. For those not familiar with the veto, it is a document lodged by one party to the adoption ie a birth parent or an adopted person, which registers that person's refusal either to be contacted or to sanction the release of identifying information.*

5. My vote on the veto

My experience with the New Zealand veto has been painful. When I tried to contact my son in 1994, he reacted by placing a veto. I was shocked and deeply disappointed.

I had not anticipated that he would place a veto, so I knew nothing of its ramifications. However, I discovered quickly that it applied for ten years and could be renewed. Alarmingly, 2004 seemed a lifetime away (it was next century, another millennium!), and beyond then did not bear contemplation. As I dug more deeply, I found out about the scope of the veto, and I became less discouraged. The veto did not prohibit contact. Rather, it prevented the relevant section of the Department of Social Welfare from releasing identifying information about my son. In other words, he was protected for ten years from the possibility of my again requesting the department to ask him to approve the release of his identifying details. As a helpful departmental pamphlet called *Adult Adoption Information Act 1985: Your Rights* explained, for adopted persons "a veto does not mean you will never be found, it just means that anyone trying to trace you won't be able to get information from this source."

This meant that, if I searched publicly available information about his adoption, I was free to find my son. As I live in Melbourne, I employed a professional based in New Zealand to search the records. Within days, she was able to give me his adopted name and the names and address of his adoptive parents, the home in which he had been raised, but had now left. Because I was apprehensive that he might have a different interpretation of the veto than the one intended, I did not contact him immediately. I waited three years, during which the need to resolve the unknown grew to the point where it became overwhelming. After seeking advice from others with similar experiences on how I might best approach my son, I called his listed telephone number. My worst fears were realised. My son resented my finding him. He was rigid in his belief that the veto he had imposed prohibited contact, period. He was not interested in my assurances that I had followed the protocols of an information veto. It was obvious he was not familiar with the *Your Rights* pamphlet. Our conversation was brief and difficult. The veto remained. *

In the aftermath of 1997, I have reflected on vetoes in general and the New Zealand version in particular. Mary Iwanek, in an April 1998 paper in *Social Work Now*, concludes, that after a decade in operation, the New Zealand system had proved to be ineffective, because many people had made contact despite the veto being in place. As I had confirmed with my experience, the availability of indexes of births, deaths and marriages, as well as electoral rolls, makes searching possible, obviating the need to seek information via the department. She also suggests that facing a veto with no accompanying written explanation often encourages rather than deters the searcher. From other sources, (which came to my attention before 1997 and influenced my actions), there is anecdotal evidence that people sometimes place the veto as a tactic to buy time. The veto is not a firm 'no', but more a deferral. In this circumstance, the person placing a reactive veto may be exercising some control over an event that they believe has the potential to overwhelm them emotionally.

New Zealand has been operating under its present *Adoption Act* since 1955. The Law Commission's 2000 review *Adoption and its Alternatives: A Different Approach and a New Framework* is an attempt to understand what needs to be changed and why. On the subject of vetoes, after acknowledging that they can be and often are circumvented, the Commission recommends that the entitlement to place new vetoes be phased out over a three year period. The Commission also advocates that the provision for existing vetoes remain, along with the option for ten year renewals.

Informed by own experience, I support the view that the New Zealand veto is not effective. Beyond the ease of circumventing the veto is the capacity for it to cause confusion and anger when the person placing the veto believes falsely that they are absolutely protected – that the veto prohibits any contact by birth parents (in my case), rather than an approach by the department. In this situation, the veto has the potential to compromise the possibility of a relationship developing between two consanguineous adults.

What the person placing the veto often protects is not their privacy, but their denial. There is an unwillingness to accept that adoption equates with loss, with, as a consequence, unresolved matters. The veto prevents this person from facing their adoption issues, from integrating them into their life and acknowledging their personal history. Those who search and are confronted by the veto are prevented from continuing their journey of discovery and recovery. The person lodging the veto blocks not only their own healing, but also disempowers the searcher and potentially retards that person's healing. It is inappropriate that a birth parent or an adopted person be given the power to hinder the other's quest to resolve personal adoption issues. Whereas other adults in the community can make choices regarding their relationships, the veto denies birth parents and adopted persons the capacity to forge a relationship, a demeaning situation based solely on the circumstance of birth.

In New Zealand, for birth parents, the legislation in effect imposes two barriers to the access of identifying information. As well as the veto, there is the requirement that the inquirer seek the consent of their son or daughter to allow the release of the data. The inquiry is made on their behalf by a departmental social worker. If a veto is in place, this approach is not made. The use of social workers as mediators conveys the impression that the searcher is incompetent and unable to be trusted. Birth parents are reminded of the disempowerment they experienced when they relinquished their children to adoption.

In South Australia, which has provision for an information veto for pre-1989 adoptions, if the veto is not in place, both adopted persons and birth parents have access to identifying information from departmental records, and with it the freedom to make direct contact with each other, without the intervention of social workers. Social workers play a more meaningful role, that of preparing the searcher for contact, should these services be sought. South Australia has but one barrier (the veto) preventing access to identifying information, and support groups are attempting to have the last hurdle removed from the state legislation.

Victoria is the only Australian state to have neither an information nor a contact veto in its adoption legislation. However, birth parents are required to seek permission for identifying information to be released. As in New Zealand, a social worker approaches the adopted person, acting on behalf of the birth parent. Thus Victoria has an inhibitive barrier, but not the prohibitive. I am a resident of Victoria and I have heard no one in the adoption community complain about the lack of a veto. I have, however, heard complaints about, and am aware of plans to seek to amend, the lack of direct access to identifying information.

New Zealand has a historical international reputation for leading social change. For example, in what was seen as a progressive move at the time, New Zealand was, in 1881, the first country in the then British Empire to legalise adoption. On the subject of the veto now in operation, however, New Zealand cannot hold its head high. Australian states such as South Australia and Victoria have shown somewhat more enlightened attitudes to the veto, those which encourage, to some degree, the mending of families separated by adoption. New Zealand, however, adheres to the mistaken belief that people affected by adoption need 'protection', when what is in fact protected is a perpetuation of the pain and suffering created by separation through adoption. What adopted persons and birth parents would benefit from is protection from, not by, the veto, so that they can deal with their adoption issues and integrate these experiences into their lives. New Zealand can go beyond the recommendations of the 2000 Law Commission report and re-establish its reputation for leading social change by 1) allowing the release of identifying information to the inquirer without the need to seek the prior approval of the person sought, and, 2) abolishing the veto.

* This was the situation when I wrote the article. When the veto my son had placed in 1994 expired in 2004, he chose not to renew it. Viewing the veto as a symbol, I welcome his decision, because it offers the possibility of a softening on his part. I recognise that, alternatively, James may now acknowledge that, in a practical sense, the veto does not

prevent contact, whilst at the same time he maintains his position that he does not want dialogue with either of his birth parents. Looking back, I maintain that the veto he placed did not afford him the protection that he believed falsely was inherent in, but never promised by the measure. I remain implacably opposed to any veto.

I was unprepared for the feelings I experienced when my grandson was born in December 2003. I felt compelled to record my reaction to this beautiful moment and to make comparisons with how I reacted to the births of my children. First published in VOICE *in the Summer Edition of January 2004, this article was also reprinted elsewhere. In the next edition of* VOICE, *there appeared two articles by grandmothers, telling of their responses to the births of their grandchildren.*

6. Reflections on becoming a grandfather

Recently, my grandson was born. My reaction was profound. I was moved. When I saw him for the first time, three hours after his birth, I responded with pure joy. I could not take my eyes off my grandson. I wanted to hold and keep holding him, so that I could appreciate his fresh smell and his softness. In particular, his tiny wrinkled fingers and toes fascinated me. A photograph taken that evening of father, grandfather and new born babe shows me beaming with sheer happiness and pride. When I came home, I could not resist ringing friends and family immediately, irrespective of time zones, so that I could share the euphoria I was feeling.

Other grandparents tell me that these responses are not uncommon. It seems that, spared from the obligations of parenthood, we appreciate the opportunity to enjoy our grandchildren unreservedly.

To give my intense reaction a context, this was not how I behaved when my children (one the mother, in 2003, of my grandchild) were born. My responses to their births almost thirty years previously were, by comparison, muted. I recall experiencing a relief that my son and my daughter had been born safely, tinged with an anxiety, because this was, for me, the beginning of the responsibility that accompanies fatherhood. After being involved in both births, I, in the aftermath, felt somewhat detached. I did not experience the unrestrained pleasure that the birth of my grandson later gave me.

I believe there are deeper factors that have influenced my differing reactions, almost three decades apart. They have their roots in my adoption experience. My children were born less than a decade after my first born son was adopted. I was not present at his birth. In the aftermath, I thought that I had put the birth and loss of my first child behind me and got on with my life. It was not until two and a half decades later that I came to terms with having fathered an illegitimate child at age 21.

Having, over the last decade, devoted much effort to exploring, understanding and coming to terms with my adoption experience, I now believe that my deadened responses to the births of my (second) son and my daughter were to be expected. When they were born, I had not acknowledged the guilt and the shame associated with the birth and subsequent loss of my first born son. I had covered these painful emotions with the blanket of denial. Although I did not accept it at the time, I carried wounds. My feeling inhibited, even numb, at the births of my subsequent children, was, I consider, a consequence of the defences I had constructed to protect me from having an emotional response to their arrivals, because any feelings were likely to be painful, guilt-ridden and potent reminders. I kept the lid on my emotions, because to do so felt safe. When my wife gave birth to our son in 1974 and two years later, to our daughter, my buried past reinforced my subdued reaction.

Now, whilst I have not completely resolved the issues surrounding the loss of my eldest son, I have been able to give them a context. I have incorporated them into my life. My wounds have healed somewhat. I can write and talk about my adoption experience, freed of the burden of shame. Coming out into the open has been a liberating, even uplifting experience. No longer do I feel the need to keep my emotions in check.

Paradoxically perhaps, I feel more in control of my life now than when I deliberately censored my feelings. Within this setting, to me it makes perfect sense that I reacted openly and without inhibition to the birth of my grandson.

There is a related, unknown element that, whilst it has not affected my recent celebrations, causes me to pause and to contemplate. I have not yet met the son I lost to adoption. He is now in his mid-thirties and married. I wonder if he and his wife have children? Perhaps I am a grandfather several times over. I may never know the answer. If my son and I do not ever meet, we will have missed the opportunity for a special relationship. If my bloodline has been passed through to the next generation and I am denied the privilege of getting to know my New Zealand grandchildren, then I know, based on my reaction to the birth of my grandson in Melbourne, that three generations will have missed out on the chance to know and to appreciate their antecedents and their descendants.

My grandparent experience has been one of wonderment, tempered a little by reflection and wistfulness. I know of one other account by a birth parent. In *Adoption and Loss: The Hidden Grief*, Evelyn Robinson writes of her differing reactions to the birth of her (to be) adopted son and two granddaughters (2003, pp222–223). It would be interesting to know about the experiences of other birth parents who have become grandparents.

After publishing my first book, I visited New Zealand with a fellow birth parent and author. My account of our successful alliance was first published in ARMS Update *in February 2005. Learning to feel comfortable about speaking in public is a part of my personal development.*

7. Working well together

Late in 2004, Evelyn Robinson and I toured New Zealand. Over twelve days, we presented a series of joint seminars about adoption issues. The audiences comprised the general public and people with adoption experiences, as well as professionals involved in the adoption and post-adoption processes. Participants welcomed our contributions. The immediate and subsequent feedback was overwhelmingly positive. Many people took away an awareness of the benefits of including all three members of the birth family – mother, adult child and father – in searching and reunion. Some people said that what we conveyed caused them to reconsider the way they viewed their adoption experience. For professionals, our presentations reinforced the value of post-adoption support and counselling to assist healing. People without adoption experiences told us that the seminars were educational.

We toured, having recently published books; in Evelyn's case her second, in my instance, the first. Evelyn had presented seminars in New Zealand in 2001, to coincide with the release of her first book, *Adoption and Loss: The Hidden Grief*, so she was already known to local audiences. I had, in the last few years, achieved recognition in New Zealand, through the publication of several articles in the Christchurch-based newsletter, *issues*. For me the trip was also a return to the land of my birth and the location where, in 1967, my son was placed for adoption.

Transparent

Evelyn was a stranger to me until I read her first book. At the time, I was struggling with the format and scope of my book, written from the perspective of a birth father. I related to what Evelyn had written and when I contacted her to provide feedback on her book, she encouraged me to publish my story and research findings. Thus, in 2000 our association began.

Traditionally, birth mothers and birth fathers have not always shown empathy with each other's viewpoint. However, Evelyn and I have discovered that we share similar views about the outcomes of adoption, so it was perhaps not unexpected that we would share a podium. As far as we are aware, our joint presentation was the first seminar held anywhere, in which the perspectives of both birth parents were aired and discussed. Our collaboration allowed us to illustrate the actions and reactions of the mother and the father, noting the similarities and the differences.

In our presentations, Evelyn was the first speaker. From a foundation of disenfranchised grief she discussed the impact of loss on the lives of, in particular, the mother and the child. Evelyn then highlighted the opportunities for family members to understand and integrate their adoption experiences into their individual lives, including the often misunderstood imperative to seek each other out later in life. As a culmination, Evelyn provided insights into the issues that accompany reunion, the subject of her second book *Adoption and Recovery: Solving the mystery of reunion*. In the course of my presentation, building on the base set by Evelyn, I examined what fathers think and feel about their adoption experiences. From these observations, the father of a child lost to adoption materialises as a discrete parent with specific feelings, to the surprise of many people.

Evelyn and I established the setting for our contributions, by, in each case, telling encapsulated versions of our adoption stories. We found that this worked well, both to engage the audience and as a framework for informing the more general considerations that followed. In one city Evelyn also presented a separate session for birth mothers. This was welcomed by the mothers, who said it had been valuable for them. In the future, I hope that there are sufficient numbers of interested men to warrant holding an equivalent session for birth fathers.

Overall, I believe that our tour was a success because, thanks to co-ordinators in each city, it was well organised and what we had to say was considered to be helpful, even ground-breaking. There is no doubt that the participants appreciated hearing the perspectives of a birth mother and a birth father in a single seminar. Further, the audiences became aware that birth mothers and birth fathers could work together effectively. Ultimately, this was not just another adoption seminar; it was different and, based on feedback, for many it made a difference.

Postscript

In July 2005, when we presented seminars in Melbourne, Evelyn and I were joined by Evelyn's son Stephen. We believe that this is the first time that a birth mother, a birth father and an adopted person have co-presented. The audiences said that they appreciated hearing the viewpoints of all three members of the family of origin.

This article is new. To coincide with the publication of Ever After: Fathers and the Impact of Adoption, *I thought it was an opportune time to reflect on the journey I have taken since 1992. I feel as though I have made significant advances, that I am now a more complete person, a sentiment echoed by the two of my children who know me.*

8. Self-exposure

As I look back from the vantage point of my sixth decade, I find I am astounded by the advances I have made over the last dozen years. I seem to have come of age. I feel more engaged by the world around me and willing to be involved. I am comfortable in my own company and I appreciate the companionship of others. My life is rewarding.

What is it that has brought about this transformation? Quite simply, it began with a determination to confront the past, to unearth the matters that had caused my personal malaise, which had lasted a quarter of a century. Events have cascaded from the salutary moment when I decided that, for me to advance, I needed to come to terms with my adoption experience. For too long I had buried what I felt about losing my first love and the child whom we had conceived. The cocoon I inhabited not only prevented me from acknowledging my grief, but shielded me from warming to and being engaged by the world about me. In my mid-forties, I realised that I was leading, nay following a shallow, shadow life. My life was constrained, my personality repressed. I inhabited an existence that seemed to be without colour or illumination. In other words, life seemed drab and to lack direction. This does not mean that I was depressed or suicidal. I simply felt unfulfilled. I was adrift.

Transparent

The moment that I began my search for those separated from me by adoption I became a man of purpose. When I discovered that Kay, the birth mother of my son was alive, I felt faint with exhilaration. The release of emotions I had long buried was cathartic. I experienced relief and saw a way ahead. I had begun the entwined journeys of finding first the mother and then the son I had forsaken 25 years previously, and discovering my authentic, unshackled self.

My personal progress has been significant and enriching. I have learnt the wisdom of the axiom that telling the truth is best, because inventing alternative versions of events is energy-sapping, confusing and damaging. My truth centred on accepting, after two and a half decades of denial, personal responsibility for the loss of Kay and my son from my life and of wounding them because of my selfishness. I had transferred much of the blame for my actions to my parents, particularly my father, whose advice and support I had sought, about my earlier than expected family.

Early in my post-1992 odyssey, I recall standing before the graves of each of my parents to tell them that I forgave them for their part in the loss of Kay and my son. At the time, my tears seemed to be therapeutic, but afterwards doubts lingered. It was not until I sought to understand the background to my actions, that absolute forgiveness of my parents occurred. I considered my upbringing, the values under which I was raised, as well as the social milieu of the mid-1960s. I realised that the views of my parents and the stigma of illegitimacy were but contributions to my concerns about having instant fatherhood thrust upon me. Rather than blaming my father for his lack of support, I accepted that against my family environment and the prevailing social climate, the choice not to stand by Kay and her then unborn child had ultimately been mine to make.

Whilst I could not achieve face-to-face settlements with my parents, I have been fortunate to find Kay again. Because of our joint commitment to honour the individual lives and partnerships we have forged, communication between Kay and me has been limited. Nevertheless, we have managed to discuss the factors that caused the family we had pledged ourselves to establishing to be split asunder, as well as the ramifications of our three way separation. I am blessed by Kay's dedication to telling the truth about how she felt when I renounced her and our unborn son, and the impact that the loss of our incipient family has had on her life. Without her honesty, my progress would have been stifled. Kay has told me that my openness with her has assisted her to process her loss and her grief. I am pleased that I have, since 1992, in some measure, been able to help her. The third member of our birth family, our son, has chosen not to know either of his birth parents. It seems probable that he has not yet accrued the benefits of recognising, then addressing the issues associated with his separation from the two persons who gave him the gifts of life and love. I am concerned that he may be stuck where I was, more than a decade ago. For his sake, I would like to approach him and offer what I have learned from my journey. However, I refrain, because I respect his right to make his own discoveries, if and when he chooses to do so.

Addressing the pain of severance from Kay and my son has given me the freedom to explore the other avenues of my life. The primary beneficiary has been the relationship with my other two adult children. When they were infants, children and then teenagers, I was an emotionally distant parent, incapable of giving of myself fully. A change in the tone of our relationship occurred when I told them, as young adults, of their older half-brother. It was as if the fog had lifted. Today, we communicate without inhibition on many levels. Their marriages in 2002 and 2003, followed by the birth of a grandchild, have been amongst the highlights of my life, many of which, I notice, have been concentrated in the last decade.

Putting my adoption experience into context has allowed me to deal with the sadness of the 1999 divorce from my wife. Further, it has given me the confidence to make a career change, a consequence of which has been increased job satisfaction. Another benefit has been the insight I have gained into the experiences of others who have been separated by an adoption. At support groups, listening to others articulate their pain has validated my experience. It has helped me to expose my own feelings and to provide them with a setting. There is no doubt that one of the most significant steps I have taken on my journey of self-discovery is the decision I took to attend support group meetings. Here, I have felt that I was among people who understood my predicament, just as I have come to empathise with theirs. It is a relief to know that I am sharing my journey with others who have pursued parallel paths. I have found that the more I have listened to and read about how an adoption has affected other participants, the better I have come to comprehend not only my own adoption experience, but also what my son might be going through. Whilst I do not know my first born son, I feel that we have a bond. Beyond our consanguinity, this connectedness is due also to my having gained an inkling of the dilemmas that confront adopted persons. I am certain that James is a special person to know, to a degree, perhaps, because of the genes he has inherited!

As well as absorbing the adoption experiences of others and telling my story orally, I have found that writing about my experience and the consequences of adoption is therapeutic. For many years now I have kept a journal. In the exploratory days of my journey, entries were frequent and likely to convey some angst. Recent entries have been spaced and they reveal the well-being I now feel. My increased self-esteem has also allowed me to write for public consumption. Over the past five years, I have penned more than thirty articles, a booklet and now two books, all on adoption and its impact. Recently, my communication horizons have broadened to include public speaking about the impact of adoption. I have also benefited from the several personal development courses I have attended over the last decade. In a setting where the participants have been willing to expose themselves emotionally, I have appreciated the freedom to disclose my pain and my sorrow. Prior to 1992, I avoided revealing myself.

Transparent

I can identify four stages in my personal growth, which embrace a growing awareness and a preparedness to be answerable to myself. They involve personal work, against a background of tolerance and endorsement by others. The first phase was characterised by timidity, in which I feared what I had unearthed and hesitated before taking small steps. To progress, I had to steel myself and focus on the potential benefits, not the 'what-ifs'. At this time, I was an island. In the second phase, sharing my story became the imperative. In support groups, I appreciated the opportunity to tell of my pain and welcomed the validation of people with adoption experiences. In turn, hearing the perspectives of birth mothers and adopted persons was critical to my progress. During phase three, I sought to understand my feelings, to give them a framework. Here, the resources of libraries proved invaluable, particularly those books that gave adoption experiences a context and informed me about loss and grief and guilt. Applying the wisdom of others, I began to comprehend why I felt sad, and guilty about my actions, which had resulted in an adoption. In phase four, I applied what I had learned to my self. I integrated my (previously hidden, but now revealed) adoption experience into my life, a process that continues to this day. Now, I feel less isolated and more a member of the large adoption community. Whilst this final phase is the most rewarding, for me its achievement would not have been possible without the preceding steps.

I still have issues to resolve. I have not completely forgiven myself for the pivotal role I played in the separation of members of my birth family. Although I accept that it is Kay and I who share the responsibility for our son being adopted, instead of raised by us, it was my lack of support for her that precipitated this outcome. Nor have I achieved reunion with my son. I have yet to participate in his healing. He has yet to offer to help me mend further and indeed may choose not to do so. And despite having enjoyed the company of several female friends, I have found it difficult, having got close, to stay committed. It is as if I fear another shattering separation, a reminder of the one that caused me to lose Kay, my first love. Should I resolve these matters, I am sure that other challenges will emerge and my journey shall continue.

That I am in a position to make this assessment is a positive development. I shudder to think how I would feel about family, friends, my surroundings and myself if I had remained in the cocoon I had constructed about myself, as the consequence of the adoption of my son. I spent 25 years being dishonest with myself. I directed misplaced energy towards keeping my 'dreadful secret' from being exposed to myself, my children and extended family and friends. I was intent on self-preservation. My perspective was narrow. In short, I was living a lie, not a life. I have discovered that telling the truth to myself and ultimately to others is liberating. Today, I am receptive to and appreciate the joys that accompany a full life.

I urge all persons to reject the secrets and lies they may have assembled, in the mistaken belief that they are protecting themselves from the harmful effects of their adoption experiences. The harm lies in denying the truth about the impact of the experience, more than the experience itself. If you choose to bury the past, you are consigning yourself to a confined existence, beset by wariness, even distrust. It is far better, for the sake of personal well-being to acknowledge the consequences of your adoption experience and to incorporate them into your life. Just as the initial separation caused pain, so keeping your adoption experience detached from the rest of your life reinforces the loss and the grief. I maintain that it is only by acknowledging the impact of your adoption experience that you get in touch with your authentic self.

SECTION TWO

Pain and Prejudice

Transparent

"Troubles shared are troubles halved" – **Proverb**

This group of essays is about the suffering caused by the separation of birth parent and child. My writings focus on a broad view of the impact of adoption, ranging from public ignorance to the perspective of insiders. **Pain and Prejudice** *addresses such diverse topics as the meaning of Father's Day for birth fathers, slanted reporting of the consequences of an adoption and the words used to describe adoption experiences. There is also a story that does not have an adoption setting, but highlights issues in common.*

This is a short piece, which informs readers that, like birth mothers on Mother's Day, birth fathers can have problems dealing with Father's Day. The editor of issues *recognised the significance of the day for birth fathers and this article was included in what was called the 'Father's Day' edition of Sept–Nov 2002.*

1. Some thoughts for Father's Day

It has been long recognised that Mother's Day is difficult for birth mothers. This is the day when they see those around them, who are blessed by being in integrated families, celebrate the role of motherhood. For the birth mother, separated from her (sometimes only) child by adoption, the day reinforces her grief, because painful memories may be foremost. For many birth mothers, Mother's Day is anything but a celebration. Enlightened birth mother support organisations have acknowledged the significance of Mother's Day and have provided avenues for those who feel distressed to seek comfort. A well-publicised phone-in facility is sometimes used.

However, the reactions of birth fathers to Father's Day remain a mystery, and I have never heard of a phone-in being provided on the day for birth fathers. Does this mean that Father's Day has no impact on birth fathers? To assume this would be to conclude that the loss of a child to adoption does not affect birth fathers.

My experience and that of a group of New Zealand birth fathers who participated in a workshop called *Being a Birthfather* at the Canterbury Adoption Awareness and Education Trust's conference at Lincoln in February 1998, belies the commonly held belief that birth fathers do not care about the children they relinquished. We talked openly about never forgetting our children, and of our desire to know them as adults. We shared our pain and spoke of the gaps in our lives. Some common themes emerged, which we collated under the three 'Ds' of Disempowerment, Denial and Damage. At the time of the adoption, we regretted we had not been in a position to influence decisions about the future of our child, often because of the intervention of disapproving, non-supportive parents. As a consequence of feeling manipulated, a common reaction amongst our small sample was to enter a period of denial, and pursue career and other objectives, as if nothing had happened. However, the issues surrounding our forsaking of mother and child refused to remain suppressed. We had been damaged by our loss, and the guilt, shame and fear that we may never be forgiven for our deed needed to be addressed before we could move forward.

Studies of birth fathers undertaken in the last decade in Australia and the United Kingdom support these views. Again the sample is small, with a maximum of thirty participants each for two of the studies by Cicchini (1993) and Clapton (2003), reflecting birth fathers' tendency to remain in the shadows (perhaps the appropriate collective noun expression for us is 'an absence of birth fathers'!), but two themes emerge. For these birth fathers, the legacy of adoption is a permanent scar and they care about the children they lost.

Birth fathers who participated in these studies report that the long term effects of losing their child include their views of themselves, as well as the impact on their roles as husband or partner, and father. Some speak of experiencing a succession of unfulfilling, disrupted relationships. A number of birth fathers are so disgusted with their adoption experience that they opt not to have any more children.

A persistent thread in the narratives of these men is their exclusion from decisions about the future of their child, because the birth mother and/or her parents took control. Those placed in this situation refer to feeling powerless, and ashamed of 'not being there'. Other birth fathers rue that they had chosen to withdraw from the decision-making, ignorant of the ramifications of their ill-considered action on the birth mother, their child and themselves. Many, expressing guilt and sorrow, regret that their past mistakes cannot be undone. These birth fathers say that they think about their child frequently. They wonder about how he or she is faring. Curiosity and a desire to explain the circumstances and reasons for the relinquishment are common reasons provided by birth fathers for initiating a search. These feelings typically have increased over time.

So, on Father's Day, please acknowledge that out there are birth fathers who will be thinking of the children they lost to adoption, lamenting the circumstances that allowed separation to occur, and hoping that their son or daughter is sparing a thought for them.

This is another new article, which I wrote in 2005, as a reaction to the common misrepresentation in the popular media of the outcomes of an adoption.

2. The saccharine view

In the three decades after World War II, the perception that adoption was a panacea held sway. This was the era of the post-war baby boom, which coincided with, according to Harkness,

> "a strong societal push to re-establish normal family life. Marriages had been postponed during the war while women did the jobs normally held by men. Women were pressured to give the jobs back to the men, get married and have children. The nuclear family was increasingly looked upon as 'the norm' and motherhood became the highest expectation of most married women" (1991, p11).

In a society that championed marriage and children, it is to be expected that childless couples felt pressured to conform. Adopting a child and treating him or her as if they were naturally born to them allowed couples unable to conceive children to conceal their infertility. Just as a few decades later Microsoft was invigorated by their belief that every home needed a personal computer, so the credo of this post-war era was 'a child for every married couple'. Adoption became a way of meeting adult needs; the interests of the child were secondary. One adult misfortune, *ie* an out-of-wedlock birth, resolved another – childlessness.

Thus evolved the fable that an adoption provided advantages for all participants. For the birth parents, it removed the stigma of an unplanned, inconvenient pregnancy. Adoption provided an instant family for adoptive couples and for a child it removed the stain of illegitimacy and gave them a permanent childhood home, blessed by two parents.

A booklet produced in 1958 for newly recruited social workers in New South Wales, Australia, mirrors the then prevailing attitudes:

> "Adoption is one of the most satisfying of the Department's activities. The natural parents of children surrendered for adoption are unable to provide their children with the normal home environment of mother and father living in harmony, which is every child's right. Legal adoption is a means of ensuring these advantages from birth, provided satisfactory standards of investigation and placement are observed. Adopting parents on the other hand are provided with a means of establishing normal family life within their home, and it is a constant source of pleasure to officers of the Department [of Child Welfare and Social Welfare] when adopting parents proudly bring their children to head or district offices and enthuse over their progress" (Harkness, 1991, p14).

A rosy view of adoption is the one, that today, still holds sway in the popular media. In the decades since World War II, whilst the emphasis among the adoption community has shifted from the integrated adoptive family, to the parent and child separated by an adoption, this has not translated generally to an interest in the wider community about the impact of adoption on the participants. Rather, the public craves and appreciates stories with a positive slant about search, reunion and reconciliation, *ie* 'happy ending' narratives. People are intrigued by how alike children and their (birth) parents, as well as siblings, can be. Coincidences that occur as elements of reunion stories seem to be particularly fascinating – the parent and child who began their searches for each other simultaneously, lived in the same suburb without knowing that they were near neighbours, pursued similar careers and interests, had cats with same name, etc.

Myths are attached to all members of a family of origin. The popular misconception is that an adoption severs the original ties forever. Adopted persons are perceived to be grateful for their placement with a two parent family. Birth mothers are believed to have willingly surrendered their children. The birth father is portrayed as the cad, the callous man who sowed his seed and moved on, deliberately. There is a perception that reunions represent the joyful resolution of the original separation. These are the stereotypical views that often underpin stories about adoption in the media. As noted by Stromberg (2002, p14, in a quote attributed to Wegar, 1997, pp107–108), "public perceptions are shaped by the way reporters frame or select stories" and, as a consequence, "the human-interest element is dramatized while possible structural causes and solutions remain hidden."

Together at last is an example of the cosmetic approach. Published in *The Herald Sun* of 22 December 1998, the article begins: "Ivy Simpkins met her sister yesterday – after a lifetime believing she was an only child. The extraordinary story of a sad past hidden by two families for decades emerged when a clairvoyant warned the 84-year-old grandmother that her mother had died with a dark secret." Their meeting is described: "Within minutes of animated chatter, they discovered they had lived a street apart in their beloved Collingwood" and "Seated together on a couch yesterday as long-lost sisters, Mrs Simpkins and Mrs Glossop spoke in turn, each filling in the other's missing knowledge." The article concludes, "The women were uncertain yesterday about where their new relationship would lead them, but were content that they had found each other in time to enjoy their twilight years."

Occasionally, stories of reunions that failed to meet expectations are published. *Mum's Christmas presence turns sour, but all things are relative*, published in *The Age* on 3 January 2004, uses humour to describe what was supposed to be the adopted person's "joyful reunion with his mother, Betty", but which became bitter because of the behaviour of the two daughters she had brought with her. Their drinking, smoking and swearing was not appreciated by the son. The story is accompanied by a cartoon showing two inebriated sisters being carried away under a sign that reads "Xmas Returns."

In neither of the above examples is the wisdom of adoption challenged or the effects of the loss explored. These articles and others of their kind do not seek the story behind the story; how the persons involved came to be in the situation reported and most importantly, what are the repercussions of separation and reunion within a family of origin and for the child who grows up in an adoptive family.

Sometimes, the headline masks the content of the article that follows. *The Saturday Mercury* published *Happy Families* on 12 June 2004. The sub-headline tells the reader that "The number of [Australian] children up for adoption has dramatically declined, leaving desperate couples to look overseas for an instant family." The feature concentrates on the process of adopting a child from another country, and concludes with a summary of adoption information access rights in Tasmania. It becomes clear that the headline is misleading, for the reader is warned that "if you're adopting, say, a five-year-old child from a major capital city in another country, that child may already be emotionally damaged" and referring to communication between the birth and adoptive parents, "Many people start out saying they will (have ongoing contact) but it doesn't always continue because it can be too painful and they withdraw ..." In my view, the full headline creates the impression that implanting a child from another place creates a made-to-order family and that joy is guaranteed, forever. Patently, this is not the case, whether it be Australia or elsewhere.

In recent years, drawing on the appeal of movie stars, several articles about 'celebrity adoptions' have appeared. One piece, in *The Age* of 13 July 2002, headlined *They're cute, they're small, they're all the rage: having babies Hollywood style*, includes the comment that "Now the off-the-shelf symbol of stardom is an adopted baby." Calista Flockhart, Diane Keaton, Michelle Pfeiffer and Angelina Jolie have all opted to adopt. Any reservations expressed in the article centre on the background to the placements, not the practice of adoption. In the case of Angelina Jolie, her baby Maddox is the product of a multi-million dollar industry in Cambodia, dedicated to feeding a predominantly American appetite for quick adoptions. Purportedly, the birth mother was paid to hand over her son to an orphanage, where Maddox was first seen by Jolie.

In 2004, a novel called *Brother & Sister*, written by popular British author Joanna Trollope, was published. It is the story of adopted siblings, David and Nathalie, who decide to undertake concurrent searches for their birth mothers. In particular, Trollope explores the impact of their searches and reunions upon their respective extended families and work associates. What starts promisingly and in places displays insightfulness about the impact of adoption and the benefits of reconciliation, does, in the end become shallow, in part because the author has focussed on too many characters. More critically, Trollope falls for the trap of assuming that a brief reunion provides closure for birth parents and adopted persons, in the aftermath of which adopted persons choose between birth and adoptive families. After the reunion, she implies, the birth parents return to their 'boxes' and continue as if they are no longer part of their adopted children's lives. Beyond the world of fiction, reunion rarely provides an instant resolution of the issues that precipitated the search. Furthermore, many adopted persons maintain and are enriched by continuing contact with both their birth and adoptive families.

An example of insensitivity (and bias) comes from America, albeit not via the printed medium. In 2004, a sixteen year old pregnant girl was the focal point of the latest in the 'reality' fad: a made-for-television adoption. A summary of what took place was shown on *60 Minutes* (GTV-9) on Sunday 9 May, 2004. In what is described as bidding for a baby, prospective adoptive parents are shown visiting the mother-to-be, Jessica. They promote their suitability to participate in an open adoption arrangement, in which the adoptive parents control the degree of access that the birth mother has to her child. After each meeting, in which Jessica sets what seem to be largely closed questions, she discusses for the viewers the pros and cons of the just departed potential adoptive parents. Jessica admits to 'playing God'. One couple discount themselves by suggesting that when the birth mother came calling, the child would be told that the visitor was his 'aunt'. Later, Jessica is shown in tears, holding her new-born baby. Three days after the birth she signs the consent papers, to the accompaniment of the adoption agency worker saying "You're doing this because you love him and you want him to have a good life." The successful adoptive parents, the McKeens, record their reaction: "We'd finally gotten what we'd been looking for", as if their adopted infant was the house or the recreational vehicle they coveted. On screen, at no point were the ramifications of the loss of her child and the grief that she would experience explained to Jessica. Nor were the alternatives of parenting within the family explored. The birth father did not rate a mention. The adoption was portrayed as a desirable fait accompli, a transaction that benefited Jessica and the McKeens. In my view, none of the adult participants in the made-for-ratings programme deserved to be the parents of the infant boy. The interests of the child were not held paramount. If the child is ever told the truth about the circumstances of his adoption, he will learn that he was given away on national television. This is behaviour that nobody calling themselves a caring, responsible parent can condone. Furthermore, I believe that Mother's Day was the most inappropriate day of all to show this programme.

I am sure that these saccharine, unrealistic, but popular perceptions of adoption are replicated in newspapers and on television screen throughout the western world. For the public, there are serious ramifications, for the sugary coatings applied to such stories ensure that the consumers are spared the truth. As a consequence, the reader and the viewer avoid any uncomfortable feelings, which further distances the community from persons with adoption experiences.

Often, people are unaware of or ignore the impact of adoption. Michael Bloomberg, mayor of New York was reported in *The Age* of 13 September 2004, as saying at the third anniversary of the terrorist attacks on the twin towers of the World Trade Centre: "There is no name for a parent who loses a child, for there are no words to describe this pain." "Try birth parent," I found myself mouthing.

Occasionally, however, serious, thoughtful, well-researched articles about the consequences of adoption do appear in the press. One of these was *The Stolen Generation*, published in *The Age* on 15 June 1996. The sub-heading sums up the content, *viz* "Mothers who were forced to relinquish their babies during Australia's adoption boom say it was like being told the child was dead. Many still suffer." In the January 1992 edition of *ITA*, an article called *Adoption: Ultimate Rejection?* was published. It tells the story of Suzanne Sterling, whose world, according to the sub-title, "was shattered when she heard she'd been adopted. But there were 30 years of anguish before she met her natural mother." Suzanne describes how she felt when she found out she was adopted ("[her] sense of trust was completely shattered"), the stages of her search and reunion and the feelings that unravelled.

Sometimes those who write openly about their grief and their pain are accused of wallowing, morbidness or self-indulgence, of not getting on with their lives. More enlightened readers may recognise the sincerity of the narrator and acknowledge the benefits of emotions released and shared.

Whilst honest appraisals of the impact of adoption are welcome, unfortunately they are rare in the written media. The outmoded belief that an adoption benefits all participants continues to dominate the perceptions of the community at large. This base dishonesty may fool the general public, but it dishonours those with adoption experiences, who know the truth and the pain. To correct the myth that adoption is a panacea, I believe that it will require many birth parents, adopted persons and adoptive parents to tell their stories in their own words in the popular press. As noted by Stromberg, "self-narratives are a powerful mechanism for portraying a message and raising social awareness" (2002, pp28–29). For these narratives to be accepted and published with the integrity of the original submission preserved, the co-operation of editors with a social conscience is required. Television producers, unfortunately often reliant upon the visual happy 'grab', may take a little longer to convince that adoption equates with loss and anguish.

This tongue-in-cheek brief article appeared in VOICE *in the Winter Issue of July 2002. Of my writings, this is the one that was fun to write, because of the word play involved. However, do not be deceived by the apparent light-hearted tone, for my underlying message is deadly serious.*

3. Disturbing adoption

In the last edition of *VOICE*, Michelle Richards used the term displacement to describe her separation from her heritage. I was struck by this being another dis- word used to describe an aspect of the adoption experience, to accompany disempowerment and disenfranchised, terms I have heard used by and about adopted persons and birth parents.

It set me pondering. Are there other dis- words which apply to adoption and its after effects? Not surprisingly, given that the prefix dis- means 'lack of', 'not', or 'apart', I unearthed many descriptors that fit.

Disgrace, disapproval, discrimination, disreputable and disdain can all be used to describe how a birth mother was regarded by the community before and after the birth of her child. Those birth fathers who chose not to stand by the birth mother may be familiar with disingenuous, dishonourable and disown. Birth parents left with no option but to relinquish their child speak of being dispossessed, of having their desire to keep the child disregarded, and of feeling disillusioned with parenthood. Those whose reaction to the loss and grief caused by separation of parent and child is numbness, can relate to disengagement and disinterest. Others use disarray, distraught or disabling to describe their emotional turmoil. Both adopted persons and birth parents may distrust intimacy with others, because getting close equates with the possibility of another disruptive rejection. And many adopted persons are wary of appearing disloyal to their adoptive parents, when they contemplate the search to discover their heritage.

Because adoption has caused so much distress, should it not be stopped? If this came to pass, we could mark the occasion by coining a new, highly appropriate word – dis-adoption. And then, for future generations, all those disconcerting dis- words could disappear.

I have long admired Eric Clapton as a musician and a man of generous sprit. His interview by Melvyn Bragg on television in 1987 is one of the most fascinating I have seen or heard. In it, Eric Clapton was startlingly, refreshingly open and honest. He revealed more of himself in print in 1998 and 1999. I could not resist writing about him for VOICE *in the Winter Issue of July 2002. I have included this article, because it illustrates the impact of withholding the truth about parentage, on a person whose name is familiar to many people.*

4. Motherless child – a cautionary tale of separation and loss

Adoption has a profound effect on those caught in its web. Children who are not raised by their parents, even if the handover is not formalised by an adoption order, report experiences much in common with those of adopted persons.

Witness the story of Eric Clapton, guitar legend, multi-Grammy award winning singer, and prominent performer at the Queen's golden jubilee celebrations, who revealed his soul to *UK Mail* readers (June 1999) in an article headlined *It's hard to admit, but being left by my mother was even worse than losing my son* ... Here is a man who has suffered his share of hard knocks, activated by the first and worst of these – the discovery at age nine that his parents were in fact his grandparents, and the woman whom he thought was his much older sister was his mother. As the article goes on to say: "The young Eric had no way of coping. From that day he lost his faith in people – especially women. 'I became frightened of being lied to and of broken promises.' "

Eric Patrick Clapton was born in Ripley, Surrey on 30 March 1945. His mother, Pat was sixteen and still at school, whilst his father, a soldier named Edward Fryer, returned to Canada and his wife. When Eric was two, his mother left England for Germany with another Canadian soldier. He was left in the care of his grandmother Rose, and her second husband Jack Clapp. Eric next saw Pat in 1954, when she came to visit. He can't remember how he found out the truth, but recalls his reaction clearly: "I discovered what I thought was real wasn't at all. Up until that time I had had a very happy childhood. My feelings were of deception rather than abandonment. It was then I turned to music and began listening to the blues." He persuaded his grandparents to buy him his first guitar when he was thirteen. As Eric explained to Melvyn Bragg, he sought solace in blues music, because it represented the way he felt at the time – one man and his guitar against the world. But this was not enough to help him deal with his shattered world. He turned to alcohol and drugs.

Clapton's addictions to heroin and booze have been well chronicled. Through the turmoil he was producing memorable music with John Mayall, The Cream, and Derek and the Dominos (a thinly disguised attempt to obscure his by now famous identity), and then as a solo artist.

In 1991, his four-and-a-half year old son, Conor, fell from a tall building to his death, through a window left open by a maintenance worker. As Clapton explains: "When it happened, I felt just as I had when I was nine and found out about my mother. This time, however, ... I'd gathered enough tools to help me cope. I knew drink or drugs would not take away the pain or make me forget." He allowed people to help him, and used playing the guitar and songwriting as a part of his healing process. He dedicated the hit *Tears in Heaven* to Conor.

Since the death of Conor, Clapton has discovered a daughter he had fathered in 1983, but did not know. Ruth contacted him and asked if he'd like to get to know her. "She was very generous," he said. "We have allowed [the relationship] to develop in a natural way and Ruth has become a great solace."

Concluded Clapton in the same *UK Mail* article: "I would still like more children and think it would be a great achievement if I had a permanent relationship with a woman, but for me to even think like that is pretty much a miracle in itself. It's enough I have survived and can manage a relationship with myself." He seems to have made progress on this front, because, on New Year's Day 2002, he married Melia McEnery, immediately after the christening of their daughter.

Of his mother Pat, Eric had this to say in *The Weekend Australian* of 18–19 April 1998: "We've done a lot of work to repair bridges and come to an understanding." When she died in March 1999, Eric was at her bedside. She was unconscious when he arrived at the hospital. "It upset me that I was unable to say goodbye to her but, in a way, I was crying for me, the little boy whose mother had never been with him," he explained in the *UK Mail* article.

He never met his father, but attributes his own restlessness and fondness for travel to his male lineage. He also wonders if his father was the bloke who called on his motor bike, before his mother left. "I would like to know where he is buried, or if there is a surviving family and how we are connected," he said in *The Weekend Australian* feature.

Eric Clapton is one man who has displayed the courage to acknowledge and address the pain caused him by separation from his mother. That he has aired his feelings in public is a bonus, for this action allows those with similar experiences to identify with his reactions and responses, and thus help them address the stigma of 'being different'.

As a birth father, I am heartened in particular by the openness displayed between Eric and Ruth, the daughter he did not know he had fathered.

NB: Other notable persons who were born out of wedlock include Leonardo da Vinci, Paul Gauguin, Jack London, and Lawrence of Arabia, all restless and talented people.

Postscript

A few months after my article was published, a short article in Melbourne's broadsheet newspaper revealed that actor Jack Nicholson's beginnings are similar to those of Eric Clapton. "The woman he thought was his sister June was really his mother. She was a showgirl who got pregnant at 17. Her mother was horrified and convinced June to break off the relationship and pretend baby Jack was her mother's. So Jack grew up believing his grandmother and ... grandfather were his parents" (*The Age*, 2 January 2003). I wonder if Jack and Eric have ever met ... ?

Transparent

SECTION THREE

Cut to the Core

Transparent

"If one tells the truth, one is sure, sooner or later, to be found out" — *Oscar Wilde*

This, the middle portion of the book, contains a series of articles about the specifics of the impact of adoption. **Cut to the Core** *highlights the dangers of using emotionally charged words to describe feelings, as well as the risks of not being open with oneself and others, contrasted with the benefits of being transparent, relevant to all with adoption experiences. In the last essay, I focus on birth fathers. I contemplate their inconspicuousness and suggest some strategies to increase their involvement in searches and reunions.*

Two loaded words has not been published before. I wrote it in response to the prevalence of the emotive words 'abandonment' and 'rejection' in the literature about post-adoption experiences. I decided that it was time these destructive feelings were given a proper context. I found that I was able to relate the findings to my circumstances.

1. Two loaded words

Abandon	*Reject*
to give up entirely; relinquish; discard; desert	to repulse or rebuff; throw away as useless or unsatisfactory; refuse to consider; dismiss as faulty; fail to show concern or affection for

Verbal and written accounts about the impact of adoption are often laced with emotive words, such as loss, guilt, shame, illegitimacy, secrets and lies. However, I doubt if there are any more loaded words than the duo of abandonment and rejection. A glance at the dictionary definitions above explains why the verbs and their associated noun forms are so explosive; they strike at the very core of separation issues, which are the foundations of an adoption and its aftermath. Even more fundamentally, they pose a potential threat to humankind's growth needs of love and belonging, as well as esteem and self-esteem. They impede the achievement of a comfortable acceptance of oneself and others and efficient perceptions of reality (Coon, 1992, p318 and p492). To put it bluntly, no one likes to feel abandoned or rejected.

Because abandonment and rejection are words associated with deep feelings of misgiving, they often convey projected misconceptions rather than facts. For example, an adopted person may believe that, because, he was not raised by his birth parents, he was given away, willingly. Adopted persons may feel that they were not good enough to keep. Zara Phillips refers to the belief she held – "that I must have been bad ... or extremely ugly and defective because my mother had given me away and my friends' mothers hadn't" (2004, p22). As a corollary, birth parents may fear that they will be rejected by the adopted person, because they allowed the child to be taken in by another family. Adoptive parents may fear that their adopted child will renounce them in favour of the birth parents. When adoptive parents do not sanction the search and reunion activities of their adult child, the adopted person can feel that they have been abandoned by parents for a second time. This was the experience of Linda MacKay, who reports that "[my adoptive parents] felt I was abandoning them and the years of love and nurturing I had received" (2005, p15). In MacKay's case, "My mother gave me an ultimatum. If I was to have contact with my birth family, I was no longer her daughter" (p16).

For adopted persons, there may be the spectre of history repeating itself. This can be manifested by behaviours that are rooted in being in control, so as to avoid, at all costs, the possibility of a recurrence of the pain caused by the initial separation. To deal with the threat of rejection, adopted persons often construct a false self, because it is easier to protect themselves from further renunciation if it is not their real self whom they expose.

Some adopted persons deliberately sabotage relationships, before they themselves are rejected. As Verrier puts it, "the Golden Rule ... of these adopted persons is 'Do unto others first that which you fear they are going to do to you' " (1993, p86). She continues: "This is often what happens in the relationship with the adoptive mother, where she is tested over and over again to see if she is going to reject the child ... This testing-out ... behavior is often an enigma for the friends and partners of adoptees" (*ibid*) and "The fear that he is unworthy makes the adoptee so very sensitive to criticism or rejection ... It interferes with relationships, jobs, and school, and often brings about the very outcome which the adoptee fears" (Verrier, 1993, p88).

Those adopted persons who choose instead to be compliant are also projecting a false self. It is not a strident persona, like that of the acting-out adopted person, but a strategy to blend in and be accepted. The compliant child often strives to be the model adopted person, particularly in the eyes of the adoptive parents, so that there is no possibility of their being 'sent back'. The pursuit of perfectionism is often a characteristic of the 'good' adopted person.

In the stories of their upbringing, many adult adopted persons refer to the 'chosen baby' story. In this narrative, the adoptive parents selected the child out of the many babies who were available. This fable was meant to make the child feel special. Of course, adopted persons, even at a very young age, grasp the concept that to be 'chosen', you had first to be 'unchosen'. In the eyes of an adopted person, this means the birth parents made the decision to give them up. Further, because of their special selection status, some adopted persons believe that they owe their adoptive parents more than if they had been born to them. As Russell observes about 'unchosen' and 'chosen', "Not only is this duality difficult for the adoptee to understand, it is also difficult for the adoptive parent to explain" (1996, p63). Frequently, the word-pairing is a misrepresentation of the background to the events that led to the separation of the birth parents and the child. Often, the birth parents believe that no choice was offered. Reassurances from adoptive parents that 'she [*ie* the birth mother] loved you so much she gave you up' (or 'to us') are especially damaging to the self-concept of the adopted person. This explanation also misconstrues the actions of the birth mother.

For birth parents, perhaps their greatest fear is that their child will not want to know them. Whether the birth parent is the one sought by the adopted person or the person initiating the search, this fear may be present. As with adopted persons, the possibility that unless they are on their best behaviour, contact and reunion may not occur or be terminated, lurks in the background.

Some birth parents feel guilty that they perhaps did not do enough to keep the child. This may be a significant factor in circumstances where the birth parent feels that the decision to relinquish the child was made by others who exercised control on their behalf, but not with their assent. In short, they were disempowered. Birth parents may believe that they were abandoned by their parents, if they were excluded from decisions made about the future of their child.

Birth parents may rue not resisting the counsel of influential others, for example their parents and social workers. With the benefit of hindsight, these birth parents, more commonly birth mothers, may wish that they had rejected the proffered advice, which may have been instead a stipulation. Rarely, if ever, would they consider that by their actions they had deliberately forsaken their child.

Some birth parents feel that they have no right to search for the child they lost through adoption – this prerogative was relinquished with the signing of the adoption papers. There is anecdotal evidence that this view, sometimes emphasised by social workers keen to protect the needs of adoptive parents, is less prevalent today.

For birth fathers, abandonment can be a significant issue. A birth father may feel that, because he did not support the pregnant mother, he forced her and her unborn child into adoption. He may believe that he abandoned not one person, but, because the mother was carrying their child, two people. He may label himself a 'double abandoner' and carry the internalised burdens of shame and guilt, until he accepts the opportunity to review the events surrounding the conception and consequent adoption.

Some adopted persons do not search because of the misconception that they were abandoned as the result of a calculated act. This may be reinforced by the perception that the birth parents cared so little for their child that they played no role in selecting suitable replacement parents; they left the child to his or her fate. These dangerous fantasies, if not countered by the adoptive parents, may cause the adopted person to reason that 'they abandoned me, so why should I care about them?' Behind this statement may lurk the unexpressed fear of 'they didn't like me the first time and they still may not like me, so I won't take a risk and check them out.'

Many birth parents are shocked to find that some people accuse them of abandoning their child. They renounce the proposition, that in losing their child through adoption, they rejected and continue to reject their progeny. To them, there is a world of difference between not wanting to keep a child and being unable to keep a child. This is expressed by Robinson: "I have never yet heard a mother or father say that in allowing their child to be adopted, they were rejecting or abandoning that child" (2004, p161). Personal, often heart-rending narratives by birth parents are filled with the pain of the separation itself and the consequences of living apart from consanguineous family members. Embedded in this hurt and grief is the concern that actions, which resulted in the estrangement of parent and child, may be misinterpreted as abandonment and rejection. As noted by Robinson, "some people interpret the other person's behaviour as rejection or abandonment, but people rarely describe their own behaviour in that way" (2004, p219). Robinson points out that if birth parents had had any idea that their actions would cause their children to perceive they had been abandoned, "they would have had more reason to resist the idea of adoption. Many of them did not resist, because they were told that by allowing their children to be adopted, they were actually doing them a great favour and showing how much they cared about their well-being" (2004, p8). It is no surprise then to find that many birth mothers (and birth fathers) later welcome the integration of the child, who was separated from them by adoption, into their lives.

I would be distressed if Kay had or James were to inform me that I 'abandoned' them, yet this reaction, putting aside the persons that they are, would, in one way, not surprise me, because it would be congruent with the way I feel about my actions of

1966–67. Feeling that I abandoned Kay the birth mother and her unborn child is the core of the guilt that is embedded in my adoption experience. Yet, I know that Kay did not and does not believe that I abandoned her. The guilt of being a 'double abandoner' is a burden that I need not carry. However, it is a belief about myself that I find difficult to cast aside. In my struggle, I find that I relate to the observation made by Butler-Bowdon: "... attached to notions which reality does not support, we lose some of our freedom" (2001, p266).

Furthermore, because my son does not wish to meet me, I have, until recent years, internalised this as his rejection of me. However, it is unusual for an individual to reject a person they do not know. Instead, the person who avoids communication is more likely to be rejecting an uncomfortable circumstance. I now appreciate that James's unwillingness to get to know me is perhaps more a reflection of his reluctance to own up to and to explore his own adoption issues. When he does so, then we may be in a position to contemplate reunion, raising the possibility of significant benefits for us both.

Abandonment and rejection may have little basis in fact, but, as perceptions, certainly they can create emotional turmoil, which may threaten to undermine fundamental relationships. As a consequence, removing the heat from the emotions that these words engender and placing abandonment and rejection in their proper context is an essential part of personal healing. Furthermore, interpersonal healing is compromised if either party brings accusations of rejection or abandonment to the reunion.

Those of you who have read Ever After: Fathers and the Impact of Adoption *will be aware that I deplore the barriers that impede personal healing. For those separated by an adoption, secrecy and denial are the two prime culprits. Here, I take the opportunity to get inside these inhibitors and to expose their insidious results. I reveal that rather than learning from previous mistakes, we are instead repeating them, oblivious to their repercussions.* Down with secrecy and denial *has not been published before.*

2. Down with secrecy and denial

Definitions and observations

Denial
   – "to protect oneself from an unpleasant reality by refusing to accept it or believe it" Coon (1992, p344)
   – "the glue that holds an already shattered self-esteem system together" Wallace (1977, p15)

Secrets/Secrecy
   – "something hidden or concealed. The keeping of a secret blocks the flow of information between people, and in this sense, it deprives them knowledge of what is true. ... secrets create a breakdown of relatedness. They undermine intimacy, they confuse and distort, they create difficult and unnecessary tensions" Krestan and Bepko (1993, p141)
   – "hidden information – that is information that is 'owed another' " and "protects something by concealing it from view" Mason (1993, p30)
   – "intentional concealment" Imber-Black (1993, p19)

– "What is kept secret often engenders shame" and "Secrets are often connected to fear and anxiety regarding disclosure" Imber-Black (1993, p19)

– "To keep a secret from someone is to block information or evidence from reaching that person and to do so intentionally. To keep a secret is to make a value judgment, for whatever reason, that it's not that person's right to possess the secret. To keep a secret requires a maze built by concealment, disguises, camouflage, whispers, silence or lies" Schooler (1995, p104)

– "Secrecy is when things about you are kept from you" Pavao (1998, p20)

– "Secrecy involves the withholding of information from those who have a considerable and legitimate stake in the situation" Hartman (1993, p102)

Introduction

Secrecy and denial pervade adoption. Denial is an internalised strategy, a way of managing and keeping at bay unpleasant matters, those which an individual prefers not to confront. Secrecy is a protective agent put in place to prevent matters of interest to others from escaping beyond the person or organisation holding the information. Both are control mechanisms that are inhibitive. They block personal growth and manipulate others.

As an element of the social fabric, legislation can condone deception and suppression. Adoption law in many western countries is deliberately shaped to maintain deceit, *eg* through the issuing of a new birth certificate, which perpetuates the myth that adopted persons are 'born' to their adoptive parents. The provision of the veto in some jurisdictions allows adopted persons (and birth parents) to practise avoidance – of their adoption issues, as well as other members of their family of origin.

Families inhabit the social fabric. Within birth and adoptive family households, secrecy may be entrenched. According to Lifton, "A family that allows open and honest communication among its members is considered healthy. A family that cuts off communication with secrecy is considered dysfunctional" (1994, p22). Secrecy can be used to divide families, as expressed by Lorbach: "To keep the secret of a child's conception means that there will always be a certain division within the family. On one side will be those that know the secret and on the other those, most especially the child, who don't" (2003, p116). For instance, in adoptive families with more than one adopted child, the parents may reveal the truth about their origins to one (enquiring) child only. They may then ask that child to withhold the information from their adoptive sibling, because they do not wish to encourage the second, often younger child to question where they came from. Howarth maintains that adoptive parents "have always held the greatest amount of power within adoption. Secrecy has been in their favour, a way of pretending their children's birth parents never existed, and they have not needed to question that secrecy – until it was challenged" (1988, p184).

I know of a situation where the birth mother, having refused to disclose the identity of the birth father to her child, has shared the information with the adoptive mother, but asked her to remain mum. Understandably, the adoptive mother feels most uncomfortable about her daughter not having information that is properly hers to receive and process. Further, she does not appreciate being asked to carry the burden of a secret.

Manipulation

Secrets have power. As expressed by Lifton, "Where there are secrets in a family system, there is a conspiracy of silence ... A conspiracy holds family members together like a negative energy force, but it also keeps them apart" (1994, pp22–23). According to adopted person Therese, "The power of secrecy remains supreme" (ARCS, 2004, p11). She explains: "It seems that I am not to know my history or that of my birth parents ... My birth mother's philosophy on this is that it is none of my business!"

Merry Bloch Jones documents the link between secrecy and shame. "Secrecy encourages the perpetuation of stigma. As long as we submit to secrecy and act ashamed, we will encourage others to condemn us and continue to live with shame" (1993, pp275–276). Robinson (2004) reinforces that for many people, adoption has "been associated with shame, secrecy and deceit" (p28). Further, "Secrets are corrosive and destructive in relationships because people are not living with reality – instead they are trying to avoid it" (p92), and "By deceiving others you are not 'protecting' them, you are actually disempowering them and retarding their growth and development" (p28). Robinson concludes that for those living with an adoption secret, the fear of sharing the information may not be about how it will affect the recipient, but actually the fear "of how it will affect your relationship with them" (2004, p213). This, she observes, is a common reaction amongst people who have been separated by an adoption – they "have a strong need to please others and to retain their approval" (*ibid*).

Sometimes secrecy can invade families without warning. Witness this story from *Further Down the Track*:

> "It was hard dealing with the reactions of my adoptive mother. I'd always known I was adopted, but she actually initiated my search by giving me my adoptive papers out of the blue a few months earlier. We talked about how she might feel if my search was successful and she seemed so supportive. But when it all happened, she was hurt and distressed – as if I had betrayed her. I found that really hard to handle, because there was so much anger and insecurity. Despite my constant reassurances, my love and fifty years of devotion to her and our family, she seemed unreachable. I was driven to secrecy. The one adoption issue I abhorred the most. Now I felt pressured to be careful what I discussed, to minimise hurt" (NSW Committee on Adoption and Permanent Care, 2001, p56).

In some families, secrets and lies may go hand in hand. Camillus, the adopted son of P L Travers, says he felt "betrayed, cheated for seventeen years", when his twin brother came calling and revealed the secret of his origins (*The Shadow of Mary Poppins*, ABC Television, 28 April 2004). Camillus' reaction reflects the undertaking made by his mother, the author of *Mary Poppins*, not to tell him that he was adopted. Ian Smith, star of *Neighbours,* revealed on *Australian Story* (ABC Television, 14 March 2005), that after being told by the mother who had raised him that he was adopted, he felt betrayed and considered that the first 54 years of his life had been a total lie.

When birth mother Gail meets her son, she discovers that "[David] had been lied to since he was a young child by being told that he'd been dumped by his ... mother" (NSW Committee on Adoption and Permanent Care, Inc, 2001, p72). Earlier, when she tried to contact her son, she was informed that her "son was a well adjusted, healthy, stable and secure young man" and that she "should not disrupt his life as contact ... would destroy him" (NSW Committee on Adoption and Permanent Care, Inc, 2001, p71). When the adoptive father does 'allow' her to see then 26-year-old David, she discovers a disturbed young man addicted to heroin, who says that the meeting is the happiest moment of his life and has questions to ask about his heritage.

At the most fundamental level, secrecy can affect the original decision to place a child for adoption. At the 8th Australian Conference on Adoption in 2004, Fiona Cameron and Jane West reported that of the 26 mothers in their study, 23 opted to keep their pregnancy a secret from their parents. Reasons cited were fear of ostracism, withdrawal of family support and shame because, in the eyes of others, they had not controlled their sexuality. These were women who lost their children through adoption and so became birth mothers. As stated by Cameron and West in their published abstract: "Compounded by secrecy, adoption becomes a solution to their predicament and many of these [birth] parents experience a profound grief that cannot be shared with family and loved ones, becoming disenfranchised in the process. Conversely, we recognise that parents are far less likely to proceed with an adoption if the pregnancy is revealed and discussed with family members" (p57).

Jones reports on the pregnancy, adoption and post-adoption experiences of seventy-two American birth mothers. Commenting on the feeling of helplessness, she reports: "Fear of discovery, anxiety about breaking society's rules, and anticipation of social stigma plagued some so badly that they condemned themselves ..." (1993, p22). Illustrating her point with the experience of one birth mother, she continues,

> "Young women like Cammy, previously unaccustomed to secrecy or deception, found that hiding their pregnancies changed them and their relationships. Trusting no one, they were unable to seek help. By the time Cammy revealed her pregnancy even to her mother, she had damaged both their mutual trust and their ability to work together to make the necessary decisions ... Her obsessions with secrecy and social acceptability left her passive and powerless, too frightened to consider the deep and permanent issue of her pregnancy" (*ibid*).

Years later, in the aftermath of the placement of their child, the women in the same study mention the stigmatisation that they experienced prior to the adoption. "Many insisted that they were damaged by their efforts to keep their pregnancies secret and claim that secrecy was considered more important than they were. In the frenzy to maintain the 'hush' around relinquishment, the needs of both birthmothers and babies were often overlooked" (Jones, 1993, p68).

Jones also comments on the reaction of immediate family members in situations where they are told about the pregnancy and adoption of the child months, even years after the event. These ranged through shock, shame, betrayal and rejection. "When this happened, birthmothers often found themselves counseling their families through phases of denial and anger, even when the denial threatened their relationships" (1993, p262). One birthmother reports the reaction of her parents to being told about their grandchild a year after the adoption – "My father didn't want to talk to me ... he was ashamed. His primary concern was keeping it a secret ... My mother was in pieces because I'd robbed her of a grandchild; my father felt that I'd dishonoured the family" (*ibid*).

Within adoptive families

From the time of the adoption, adoptive families may have encountered deceit. When placement occurred, some adoptive parents were told that the child would be theirs in perpetuity. The accompanying birth certificate appeared to prove that they were the mother and the father of this child. On occasions, adoptive parents were deliberately given misleading information about the circumstances of the child becoming available for adoption. False promises that the birth parents would not and could not enter the child's life ever again have also been recorded.

Adoption is a social construction, within which some participants prefer to maintain the deception that growing up in an adoptive family is the same as being raised by natural parents. Families who support this tenet may vigorously protect the falsehood from scrutiny. The suppression of the truth – that adoptive families are different from natural families in fundamental ways, is to employ denial. As an extreme example of this strategy, there is anecdotal evidence that some adoptive parents adopt their children from other countries, because there is less chance of later contact with the child's birth family. Here distance between often poor birth parents and the relatively affluent adoptive parents can provide a buffer for the latter. The unlikelihood of outreach by the disadvantaged birth parents may be used to reinforce the myth that the son or daughter is born to the adoptive parents. This facade becomes laughable when racial differences between the adoptive parents and the child are obvious.

There is much literature about denial as it applies within and is applied by adoptive families. Small points out that: "Family members tend to develop strategies to minimize the fact that the child was not born to the parents. In this situation, the child's basic sense of self develops around a faulty belief system. It is based on denial that there is any difference between being born to one's parents and being adopted. When this situation occurs, all of the family members unwittingly become codependents to a denial process" (1987, p36). Small notes that the codependency is similar to that observed in alcoholic families. She defines codependency as a "dysfunctional pattern of living and problem solving that is grounded in denial" (*ibid*). She then goes on to highlight the parallels between adoptive and other codependent families. These include:

- the family tries to hide the problem, around which it is structured,
- family members have difficulty expressing their feelings about the facts,
- communications about the topic are often faulty, inconsistent, confusing and emotional,
- attitudes to the adoption are rigid, and
- members of the family share a basic sense of shame or low self-esteem (*ibid*).

Summing up the characteristics of codependent families, Krestan and Bepko conclude: "Ultimately, silence rules family life. Emotional secrecy between and within family members becomes the norm" (1993, p144). Small (1987, p37) reports that a game of make-believe may be played out in a codependent adoptive family. This behaviour can be represented by statements such as: 'Your mother loved you so much she gave you up', 'As far as I am concerned my adoptive parents are my only parents', 'We told him that his (birth) parents were killed in a car accident', 'I can't tell them that I'm searching' and 'I have no interest in knowing who my birth parents are'. As summarised by Krestan and Bepko, "Lies create secrets, silence maintains secrets, and secrecy feeds denial" (1993, p142), "Maintaining these secrets feeds denial. What is hidden doesn't really exist and doesn't have to be discussed" (p144), and, as a consequence, "Real feelings remain hidden and unexpressed" (p145).

Hendrix (1992, pp128–130) is another researcher who characterises dysfunctional families – those in which the traits of secrecy and denial, a distorted sense of self and relationship problems are common. Griffith concludes: "Perhaps nothing so accurately characterizes dysfunctional families as denial" (1991, Section 13, p10). Marshall and McDonald decide that, within an adoptive family "the more the [adopted] person has been denied knowledge of their background or the opportunity within the adoptive family to discuss the meaning of adoption and its effect on the sense of belonging, the more likely the feeling of emptiness" (2001, p234). Brodzinsky *et al* observe that denial, as a coping strategy, can work for adopted persons until the first phone call from the birth mother (1993, p151). Partridge notes that, for adopted persons, "an important aspect of secrecy is the easily made assumption that if one is not allowed to know something, especially about oneself, it must be bad" (1991, p202). Hartman concludes: "A stigmatized person is protected by secrecy but secrecy also promotes stigmatization" (1993, p87). Lorbach adds another dimension – telling children the circumstances of their conception is "a measure of [the parents'] respect for them as individual human beings" (2003, p116).

Adopted persons raised in a family environment in which secrecy and denial are practised are faced with an obvious choice. Either they embrace the strategies of their adoptive parents or they elect to eschew the twin inhibitors and instead pursue the truth about the circumstances of their placement. For adopted persons who feel compelled to please their adoptive parents, this is a most difficult decision.

Birth parents remaining mum

The literature on secrecy and denial has focussed on adoptive families. By comparison, there have been few studies about secrecy and denial, as practised by birth parents. However, from birth parents who have shared their experiences, it is known that after the adoption, many became secretive about their 'status'. Some also have denied the impact of the loss of their child, and in some cases, the loss of a significant relationship with another adult.

As with their adoptive counterparts, birth parents have encountered deceit. Some have been deceived by what seemed at the time to be altruistic assurances, which proved to be hollow. It is on record that birth mothers were given assurances by family members and social workers, such as 'the child is going to a secure family environment, which you cannot provide' and 'your child is a gift to a couple who cannot have children of their own'. Physical abuse has occurred in some adoptive families. Adoptive parents have divorced; others conceive children of their own after the adoption.

Then there were the placatory claims of 'you have done the right thing for the child and yourself', 'you will forget that this ever happened', 'soon enough, you will put this behind you' and the almost universal 'you will be able to get on with your life'. Against the background of such expressions of certainty, it is little wonder that so many birth mothers felt isolated when these declarations turned out to be faulty. There is an argument that what birth mothers were told was a reflection of the social milieu of the time and that on this basis the promises are acceptable. I reject this benign interpretation. The advice, often from the lips of so-called professionals was grounded not in evidence, but in denial and hope.

There were also people who recklessly promised birth mothers permanent concealment. Against a background of perpetually evolving social attitudes, it was inevitable that such an assertion would be exposed for its fiction. Women who accepted the assurance that the secret of their pregnancy and the resultant adopted child would never be revealed have often been forced to confront the consequences of their pain and their shame later in life. "These women may feel enormous anger at having been subsequently contacted and this can interfere with them coming to terms with changing times and changed attitudes. As well as disenfranchising themselves by internalising the unresolved pain, they also disenfranchise their adopted daughter or son, more so when they will not allow any information about [the adopted person's birth] father, family relationships, health, or the beginning of the child's identity and story" (Marshall, 1999, p7).

In VANISH (2004a), 'Joy and Friends (Natural Mothers)' reflect on secrecy in adoption. They note: "From the moment most women discovered they were pregnant, secrecy entered their lives forever." They outline the manifestations – the hiding away in disgrace to protect the family from shame, avoiding the anger and disappointment of parents by moving interstate, returning to families and living within a network of lies to explain their recent absence, the deceit necessary to maintain the acceptance of friends and extended family, and withholding the knowledge of the out-of-wedlock pregnancy so that the opportunity for subsequent marriage was not jeopardised.

Because many birth mothers kept silent, it was assumed that they had actually forgotten the loss of their child and carried on with their lives as if the adoption had never occurred. What was actually a suppressed persona, was construed by the wider community to be gravitas allied with maturity. That birth mothers kept their son or daughter a secret (an illegitimate child was socially unacceptable, *ie* a bastard, in the language of the times) and buried their feelings, perpetuated the illusion that these women carried no residual issues from the loss of their child. In this surreal setting, it is little wonder that the preservation of secrets behind a wall of denial was seen by birth mothers to be socially sanctioned.

As noted by Hartman, "It was felt that the stigmatized birth mother, who had been guilty of sexual misconduct, was protected by denial and secrecy ... As soon as she signed the relinquishment papers, she ceased to exist. She not only carried a secret, but *was* a secret" (1993, pp87–88) [emphasis in the reference]. Gediman and Brown reinforce the view of a social worker who states that denial "... intensifies the birthparents' poor self image, by reinforcing the idea that what they have done is so heinous that it must forever be concealed" (1991, p14). A birth mother may also feel that she is a failure (after all, how can you be a mother and give up a baby?), if she is unable to resolve the grief associated with the loss of her child. Her misgivings may retreat deep inside, reinforcing the denial. She may carry her burden silently for years. She may even take her shameful secret to the grave.

Portuesi notes: "Denial becomes survival for most birth mothers. Frequently the ability to love or trust again is arrested. The psychological trauma may also cause amnesia around certain aspects of the experience .... when the feelings around loss are arrested, so are other feelings like anger, joy and happiness ... Life becomes muted" (2000, pp5–6). Concludes Portuesi: "The relinquishment of a child for adoption permeates all aspects of a birth mother's life" (p5). In a social environment where they felt they had few choices, the "mother-to-be often had to 'hide' as a way to safeguard her secret from friends and family" (*ibid*). Van Keppel *et al* write: "A ... factor which contributes to interpersonal difficulties is that for many, the relinquishment remains a secret – a secret they have typically kept because their family and friends may reject them were they to know. The continued support of family is often conditional on the birth mother maintaining her secret. Many have not told their husbands and other significant family members [including children]" and "... the secret many birth mothers carry has contributed to persistent feelings of isolation, alienation and unworthiness" (1987, p5). Often, a birth mother's feelings about the adoption are complicated by two factors, *viz* the loss of her child is at the same time a source of joy for the adoptive parents and there is no 'body' to associate with her grief, for the child may appear in person as an adult, asking to be re-incorporated into her life.

Birth fathers too experience a loss, similar to that of birth mothers. This is explored in Coles (2004), as well as Cicchini (1993) and Clapton (2003). Gary Clapton, writing as G Colvin in *A Cache of Feelings Buried in a Time Capsule* (1996) on the Internet, reflects on the 25 years between becoming a birth father and being found by his daughter, Jane: "... I ask myself why I did not wonder about my daughter's welfare and development in the years she was growing up? ... My daughter's adoption had little or no bearing on my life. Or so I used to think" and "[the signing of the papers] is a significant event − the significance of which is somehow buried deep underground yet still capable of causing explosions." He concludes his self-analysis: "I ask myself this: if my daughter had not got in touch with me would I have carried on believing that I first became a father just six years ago with the birth of my eldest son?" The language here is of a birth father who was in denial for a quarter of a century.

The majority of the thirty men in Cicchini's study report difficulties telling others about the relinquishment of their child. One man offered: "Most situations you have regrets about, you have trouble telling others about" (1993, p8). Another birth father was more specific: "I've lived with the knowledge that my child is out there somewhere but have pretended to the world he doesn't exist" (Cicchini, 1993, p13). Riedel, writing in Mason (1995) observes: "Birthfathers often keep their fatherhood a secret out of shame. Not speaking about the experience shuts down the grief process in its early stages and negatively impacts the development of trust, identity, intimacy, sexuality and self-esteem. A father may avoid events that remind him of the original wound, or he may deny the birthfather experience altogether by saying ... 'I never saw the child so it doesn't really exist' " (pp264−265).

According to Gediman and Brown, those birth fathers who have kept their fatherhood a secret, particularly from their wife and children, "are presented with the same dilemma that found birthmothers face: to tell or not to tell" (1991, p176). They go on to write of adopted persons who "presented themselves to birthfathers who proved unable or unwilling to tell their wives and families about the adoptee's existence. This usually is labeled 'protecting his family' and amounts to a hello–goodbye contact ..." (pp176–177).

If birth parents withhold information from immediate family, there are inherent risks. A deferred revelation ('I will tell them someday ... when the time is right') has the potential to become a time bomb. The secret may be exposed to other family members anyway, perhaps inadvertently by another person, leaving a legacy of distrust, loss of faith and perhaps anger towards the person who has held the secret. For relatives of birth parents who have taken the secret of their parenthood to the grave, the secret left behind, when revealed, perhaps by the searching adult adopted person, can have a devastating effect on the family of the deceased.

According to Hartman, keeping a secret from family and friends not only cuts off a birth parent from comfort and support, but also makes them vulnerable to exposure and shame (1993, p93). Shame, as Mason (1993, p40) points out, is a way we feel about ourselves; it is internalised; it is a "sense of being completely diminished or insufficient as a person ... A pervasive sense of shame is the ongoing premise that one is fundamentally bad, inadequate, unworthy or not fully valid as a human being" (p40). According to the same author, "... low self-esteem, anxiety, anger, depression, alienation and feelings of inferiority are symptoms of shame" (*ibid*). For birth mothers and birth fathers alike, shame is a harsh consequence of having given their child a 'better home'. This is a legacy they are unlikely to have anticipated, when given the 'usual assurances' at the time of the adoption.

There are other effects that result from denial and preserving secrets. Imber-Black notes that a secret preserved by one individual "often erodes self-esteem and one's capacity to trust other people's responses, because the secret-keeper often feels 'If others really knew, they would dislike me, disrespect me, hate me, etc' ..." Sometimes, the "secret becomes denied, repressed, and a secret even from oneself" (1993, p21).

Devoting unproductive energy to maintaining a secret has a negative effect on relationships between a birth parent (or an adopted person) and other people. Transparency and a willingness to take risks, to explore, to live life to the full, are compromised by the felt necessity to remain closed, to keep the shameful part of oneself buried. From many perspectives, denial and secrecy are counter-productive. They inhibit the growth of the very persons who hold and internalise the unnecessary burden. Like a dead weight, they impede progress. Not only is the keeper of the secret disadvantaged, but also the person from whom the secret is withheld. Being privy to the information may assist the resolution of their personal issues. The keeper of the information has no right to exercise control over the person who is the subject of the information. In the case of birth parents, this may be an unpleasant reminder of how they felt when the adoption was arranged.

When will we ever learn?

It appears that we have not absorbed and applied the lessons from adoption to the practice of donor conception, where secrecy and deceit flourish. *The Status of Children Act 1974,* under which donor conception via sperm donation takes place in my home state of Victoria, Australia affirms: "(a) the husband shall be presumed, for all purposes, to have caused the pregnancy and to be the father of any child born as a result of the pregnancy; (b) and any man, not being her husband, who produced semen used for the procedure shall, for all purposes, be presumed not to have caused the pregnancy and not to be the father of any child born as a result of the pregnancy" (Myf, in VANISH, 2004b). Myf continues: "My father was an anonymous sperm donor and for all purposes in law I am not the daughter of ... the man who made my life possible" and "if a child is conceived via donated sperm and born to a couple, the partner of the mother is assumed to be the father of that child. The birth certificate/record colludes in this deceit and unless the recipient couple choose to tell their child the [truth about] their conception, there is nothing to indicate the involvement of a 'third party' " (*ibid*). It is perhaps not surprising then that this legally condoned artifice has been reinforced by the actions of doctors, who, according to participants in Lorbach (2003), sometimes told parents to keep the donor conception "completely private and no one, including the child, would ever know" (p114) and destroyed records to protect the donors' identities (p160). In the USA, according to Cordray, "There are no names on sealed ... birth certificates located in courthouses, only coded numbers on records (if they still exist), scattered through countless doctors' offices and clinics" (2000, p12). Anecdotal evidence indicates that many children conceived through the participation of donors actually sense, without being told, that the genetic connection to the family in which they are raised is not 100 per cent. The differentiating characteristics may, for example, be skin or hair colour, mannerisms or interests. Because a donor-conceived child inherits only half of their gene pool from the parents who raise them, this matter is akin to the feeling of 'not belonging', reported frequently by adopted persons.

In Victoria, Australia, only those children born as the result of sperm or egg donation since 1 January 1998 have the right to identifying information about their biological parent. For sperm or eggs donated between 1988 and the end of 1997, information about donors is available to the offspring, but only with the consent of the donor. Prior to 1988, there was no requirement for records of donors to be kept. Donor-conceived children reaching adulthood prior to 2006 have little chance of discovering who one biological parent is. As stated by Millar, "Given the knowledge we now have about the negative effects of secrecy in past adoption practices, it is quite extraordinary that the anonymity of pre-1988 'donors' is still being protected, at the expense of their children, and that the 'rights' of donors who do not wish to be identified prevail over the children's need to know about their origins" (2001, p22). In an article entitled *The cost of secrecy –post adoption issues*, which appears on the website of The Benevolent Society of New South Wales, Australia, Margaret McDonald opines that there is a tendency here "to infantilise such offspring, avoiding the recognition of them as people who will become adults." As articulated by Lynne in Lorbach (2003), "there is no need for secrecy. Secrecy implies that the procedure is shameful, that I am shameful, that there is something wrong with me" (p186). Compounding this legally condoned secrecy is the revelation that only about 20% of donor recipients have told their children the story of their conception. This means that approximately 80% of donor-conceived children have either been lied to or had information deliberately withheld from them, by parents who purport to love them. According to Bill in Lorbach (2003), parents "often feel it is unnecessary to disclose the truth of the child's origins, believing that the child/adult will never suspect his or her paternity" (p168). This suppression may have serious consequences. Children ignorant of their origins may give false medical histories and so potentially put their lives at risk. Through denial and ignorance, the code of secrecy is perpetuated in the practice of donor conception. I am appalled by the community's inability to learn from the consequences of adoption.

Footnote

I find it ironic, that, courtesy of donor conception, after all these years, fathers are at the forefront. I speak as a birth father, a man whose child was separated from me by adoption. We birth fathers are often considered to be marginal figures in the adoption and post-adoption picture. When searched for by our children (as adults), it is often after the birth mother is found. Sometimes, because we may not be recorded on the birth certificate, we never achieve reunion with our child. For a sperm donor, there is no 'competition' from a birth mother. Should he be recorded as the donor, he is the sole person sought by his child, when he or she seeks to complete their identity. I encourage all sperm donors to allow themselves to be traced. The rewards of meeting and maintaining a relationship with your child are too important to miss.

Open remedies *complements the previous essay,* Down with secrecy and denial, *because it responds to issues raised in that article. The dynamics within adoptive families have been explored by others. Here, I focus on the means of unburdening for members of the birth family and the benefits that accrue.*

3. Open remedies

In *The Book of Virtues*, William Bennett begins the chapter called *Honesty* by drawing a comparison with the antithesis: "To be honest is to be real, genuine, authentic, and bona fide. To be dishonest is to be partly feigned, forged, fake or fictitious. Honesty expresses both self-respect and respect for others. Dishonesty fully respects neither oneself nor others. Honesty imbues lives with openness, reliability, and candor; it expresses a disposition to live in the light. Dishonesty seeks shade, cover, or concealment. It is a disposition to live partly in the dark" (1993, p599).

Within the specific context of adoptive relationships, Robinson observes (2004) "The path to emotional well-being requires honesty" (p92) and "The truth offers an opportunity of living authentically and confronting reality. The truth may cause life to seem more complex than it had previously appeared, but, in actual fact, often it was the previous deceit and/or ignorance which caused the difficulties, not the revelation of the truth" (p172). Russell summarises the pitfalls of suppression and the benefits of the substitute: "Any secret has the potential to cause harm and hurt feelings ... Secrets block open communication and create feelings of mistrust between people and in families. The truth truly does set one free" (1996, p58). Lifton echoes these sentiments, when she writes: "Once the denial and secrecy are lifted, everyone has a chance to be liberated" (1994, p269). As a reinforcement of these views penned by people with adoption experiences, it is encouraging to note from Stromberg's thesis that some of the birth fathers who participated in her study requested that they not be accorded anonymity – "... the culture of adoption has been plagued with secrecy for so long that a desire to break through the secrecy was symbolic and significant ..." (2002, p41).

In a similar vein, I applaud the stances on secrecy and anonymity taken by Stephen Ferguson (2005). Stephen was raised in an adoptive family in which "I was not supposed to tell anyone else of my alternative beginnings for fear of embarrassing [my adoptive parents] into an explanation. I played the game for a while but seeing no need to keep the information out of the public domain, I gave up and started telling people the truth about who I was and where I'd come from, as far as I knew it at the time." As an adult, after donating sperm and initially requesting anonymity, he later re-evaluated his position, "understanding [that donor conceived children have] the same desires for identity that adopted people have." As a result, Ferguson continues, "I look forward to the day that I can stand face-to-face with one or more of the people created using my sperm and explain to them how my decision helped bring them into the world. I only hope that the parents ... have the foresight, knowledge and respect to tell their children where they came from and maybe even try to help them trace me one day."

In some situations, the social stigma associated with, for example, giving up a child to adoption may be compounded by a hypervigilance. The imperative to keep the original deed a secret may be accompanied by self-protecting isolation. Before the burdens of concealment can be ameliorated, the many protective skins that have accumulated need to be peeled away. In such circumstances, the assistance of a counsellor may be invaluable and provide relief. Evelyn Robinson describes the post-adoption grief counselling she has practised in South Australia. Birth mothers have sought assistance in the first place because, for many, the events leading up to and beyond the adoption had been kept hidden, often with significant consequences. "Sometimes the secrecy had become a debilitating, entrenched factor in their lives" (2002, p58). Further, Robinson points out, "... a number of women had been led to believe that grieving for the loss of their child was itself a sign of inadequacy on their part, making them reluctant to admit to their ongoing pain" (*ibid*). Their grief is disenfranchised, defined by Doka (1989) as occurring when the loss is not socially supported, openly acknowledged or publicly mourned. As Robinson observes, "Because it is disenfranchised, the grief of mothers who have lost children in this way is usually suppressed" (2002, p58). She then outlines the steps required to address disenfranchised grief. These include accepting that grief is a healthy and expected response to a significant loss, as well as acknowledging the disempowerment that many women experienced at the time of the adoption. To increase their feelings of empowerment and self-worth, Robinson encourages the mothers to review the values and beliefs they absorbed when children and adolescents and to recall the family and community attitudes that culminated in the loss of the child. Summing up, Robinson says: "Considering that many mothers come to [counselling] feeling guilty and ashamed about having become pregnant, about having allowed their babies to be adopted and also about the fact that they are still suffering from their loss, this [understanding and acceptance of their feelings] is often felt to be a major achievement" (2002, p61). Of course, only those women who have acknowledged that they require support place themselves in a position to profit from these insights. As is pointed out by Robinson, "The aim of counselling women who have lost children through adoption is to assist them to integrate their adoption experience into their lives. Counselling focuses on acknowledging that the pain will be ongoing, while stressing that it can be managed in order that its effect becomes less and less debilitating" (2002, p59). Robinson concludes: "For many of those involved in adoption, there has been a suppression of grief which has been damaging. The services of an aware and sensitive counsellor, combined with the support of their peers, can assist those affected to overcome the negative consequences and feel the sense of relief and freedom that comes with honest and productive grieving" (2002, p62). Here empathy and professional skill are helping birth mothers to mend.

Whilst it is not essential that the counsellor have an adoption experience, it is important, to supplement their skill base, that they have some understanding of the emotional impact of an adoption upon the participants. For those counsellors who do have an adoption experience, if they have not performed personal work on themselves, their own unresolved adoption issues may intrude upon the collaboration with the client.

A professional counsellor certainly can help people to heal, but the unavailability of this guidance should not deter those affected by loss and grief from helping themselves. Great personal satisfaction and achievement can ensue from embarking on your own voyage of release and enlightenment. However, it is unlikely that advancement can be achieved by you in isolation – the encouragement and understanding of others is critical for progress. The resources provided by support groups, particularly the qualities of empathy and validation, can facilitate breakthroughs.

Focussing on birth fathers, Riedel, in Mason (1995), defines what these men need to do to break out of the cycle of secrecy and denial. He designates the stages as:

- Naming the Wound – "Only when his secret is revealed and witnessed by others, can healing begin",
- Remembering the Experience – "To move beyond powerlessness, anger and shame, a birthfather must remember." When he can share his story and his feelings, "he will begin to reclaim what happened as a part of his past, allowing him to reach some resolution to his grief" and
- Reclaiming Yourself – "When a birthfather can say 'I really did care. I did the best I could', his negative view of himself fundamentally shifts to a more positive perspective... Whether

or not a reunion occurs, healing for the birthfather requires that his memories and feelings be integrated. Only then is he free to move on with his life and begin growing again" (pp265–266).

These steps do not sound dissimilar to the incremental counselling described by Robinson above, nor to the stages outlined by Small for adopted persons.

The first stage of the (Small) process of letting go of denial is characterised by an emerging awareness and enlightenment. In stage two, adult adopted persons "begin to address some of the core issues and feelings that relate to their adoptive status" (1987, p40). Integration, in which confusion is laid to rest and the adopted person comes to terms with their authentic self, is stage three.

Van Keppel *et al* (1987, p5) conclude that, for the birth mother, whilst her loss cannot be fully resolved until she has made contact with her adopted child, there are other ways in which she can promote her adjustment. Drawing on earlier research, they note that the birth mothers who had been able to talk about and express their feelings about their loss in an environment where support was forthcoming from family and friends made a better adjustment to the loss of their child than those who felt unsupported and kept their relinquishment a secret. There are elements of acceptance and relief here for those who have shared their secret.

'A Birthmother' (VANISH, 2004a) observes, "I eventually discovered that harbouring secrets takes considerably more energy that it does to reveal the truth. And now that the secret has been revealed ... I feel as if the weight of the world has been lifted from my shoulders. I have given myself a gift that no amount of money can buy and that is ... peace of mind." On the decision to open up, Gediman and Brown comment: "Throwing off the burden of secrecy can be one of the most healing and exhilarating aspects of reunion for birthmothers" (1991, p15).

This is what an adopted person had to say about she and her birth mother both being open: "We ... experienced the peace that comes from unburdening secrets and dealing with unresolved issues. We went through the process of confronting the past and the present. We faced the reality that the future is really how we deal with the now" (NSW Committee on Adoption and Permanent Care, Inc, 2001, p58).

Whilst the above examples confirm the benefits of honesty and openness, they also exhibit the necessity of another quality – personal responsibility. Peck is one author who proclaims the need for accountability. "We cannot solve a problem by hoping someone else will solve it for us ... **we** must accept responsibility for a problem before we can solve it" (1990, p32) [my emphasis added]. According to Bennett, "Responsible persons are mature people who have taken charge of themselves and their conduct, who *own* their actions and *own* up to them – who *answer* for them" (1993, p186) [emphasis in the reference]. Peck also highlights the virtues of honesty: "By their openness, people dedicated to the truth live in the open, and through the exercise of their courage to live in the open, they become free from fear" (1990, p65).

Synthesising the various views stated above, I believe the following four stages represent the healthy evolution of a person with an adoption experience:

> *Acknowledgment*: The individual accepts that adoption causes pain and loss. For some people, this means a rejection of the denial they may have practised for years. There are parallels with other situations. For example, it is generally accepted that for alcoholics, admission of their alcoholism is the first step to recovery. Self-disclosure may be accompanied by a desire to share one's personal experience with others who have similar stories to tell. Their support and endorsement are helpful at this point. However, those birth parents and adopted persons who habitually attend

support groups and come to rely upon them purely to narrate their circumstances and seek comfort may consign themselves to remaining stuck in this phase for months, even years.

Responsibility: To move forward, the individual takes personal responsibility for their feelings, as well as any past actions that have contributed to their present situation. Taking personal responsibility is the perfect antidote to the propensity of some to blame others for their status, *eg* being adopted, and perhaps the way they feel about themselves, others and the state of the world. You cannot alter the events that are the foundation of your adoption experience, but you can change the way you think and feel about them.

Understanding: Acknowledging that adoption has affected your life and assuming personal responsibility are significant advances. However, to make further headway, I believe that the individual has to move beyond these two validation stages. In my view, the best way to progress is to explore the meaning of your adoption experience and to challenge your beliefs about that experience, as well as the community-based stereotypes. It is helpful to try to find out why you feel the loss of the other members of your family of origin and to comprehend the background to your fears, your anger, your guilt. It is useful to explore the social environment at the time the adoption took place. This delving is for one purpose – to give your adoption experience a realistic setting. You may find that, as a result of this probing, many of your earlier perceptions about yourself and others prove to be false. Furthermore, by working on and understanding your adoption experience, you have the capacity not only to realise your self-potential but also to communicate your insights, for the further benefit of others.

Healing: Whilst you can never forget about being separated from your family of origin, it is possible to incorporate your actions and reactions, which now have a context, successfully into your life and so achieve a measure of equilibrium. Those who do not begin the journey at all are destined to live lives in which their adoption experience is a separate, often buried part of a fragmented existence.

Selecting the most suitable resources to aid mending can be important. However, the key action is the one taken by the individual when he or she decides to confront perceptions based on denial, withheld information or misinformation, which are all manifestations of dishonesty. For this voyage of enlightenment and integration to begin, advance and succeed, there must be an absolute dedication to openness and honesty. Self-respect and the capacity to live an authentic life are the rewards. Without this personal commitment to address issues affecting the self, an individual's advancement is stifled. As noted by Peck, "Problems call forth our courage and our wisdom; indeed they create our courage and our wisdom. It is only because of problems that we grow ..." (1990, p14).

This essay is devoted to birth fathers. In it, I ponder the reasons for the near invisibility of men who have fathered children lost to adoption. I discuss the benefits of birth fathers becoming more accessible to themselves and to others. I advocate the participation of these men in reunion, both as the instigators and the recipients of outreach.

4. Where have all the birth fathers gone?

Preamble

In her thesis, Stromberg writes: "The shift [over the past twenty years] from closed to open adoptions has had a significant impact on the role of birth fathers in adoption. Open adoption has allowed birth fathers more of an opportunity to not only participate in the adoption plan for their child, but to sustain a relationship with their child over the years that follow" (2002, p77). Whilst I welcome this increased involvement of birth fathers, my focus is upon the majority of birth fathers who are the product of that earlier era, when freedom of interpersonal contact was denied in the aftermath of an adoption.

The invisible men

In 2000 and 2004 I attended the Seventh and Eighth Australian Adoption Conferences. On each occasion I was the sole birth father registered as an attendee. To put it another way, I was the only birth father among a combined total of more than 400 participants. I did not feel out of place or unwelcome. Rather, my involvement was commented upon favourably by the overwhelmingly female gatherings. However, the question I find myself asking is, "Where are all the birth fathers?"

The invisibility of birth fathers has been confirmed for me elsewhere. Articles written by journalists about my experience have appeared in the press. I have told my story and findings about the impact of adoption on birth fathers over the radio, yet in almost every case, it is others with adoption experiences, not birth fathers, who have corresponded with me. The response to a summary of my adoption story, which appeared in *The Age* on Father's Day in 2002, is instructive. Of the four men who asked me to contact them, one was an old school friend. When I followed up with the other three men, all, I discovered, were birth fathers. Their responses were fascinating and perhaps representative. One welcomed contact and we met subsequently. A second birth father arranged to meet me, but did not keep the appointment. When I called him later, he admitted that he had defaulted, because he had realised he was not yet ready to share his adoption experience. The third birth father said he was 'still thinking about it' and would call me when he was ready. I have not heard from him since.

When I toured New Zealand in late 2004, only two birth fathers attended the five seminars I presented in four cities. They were among the approximately 10 per cent of men, overall, who attended the gatherings. One of the birth fathers observed that he had found that once he began sharing his adoption experience with others, his circle of friends changed. He now spent less time with men, but had broadened his range of female acquaintances. He told me that other men had questioned the wisdom of his acknowledgment of the past. The other (younger) birth father maintained contact with his child and the adoptive parents. He found it somewhat difficult to relate to the experiences of birth fathers who have been separated from their children for decades, but he acknowledged at the end of my presentation that his eyes had been opened.

In Australia, since the mid-1960s there have been approximately 70,000 local placements to adoptive parents who are strangers to the child. This means there are, give or take a few, for multiple paternity and death, as a minimum, an equivalent number of birth fathers alive today in Australia. Men who conceived a child forty years ago, would, now, in general, be in their early sixties. There are likely to be, given the number of adoptions that occurred in the twenty years immediately following World War II (before the peak years of the late sixties and early seventies), additional birth fathers living from this earlier period, supplementing the 70,000 referred to above. In the United States, the 2000 census recorded over seven million adopted persons (Griffith, personal communication, 2005). These are the children of an equivalent number of birth fathers. How is it then that birth fathers are nigh but invisible to the public?

That birth fathers were historically not required to be recorded on the original birth certificate provides a partial answer. It is reasonable to assume that many of these fathers were not informed by the birth mother of their paternity, either to protect the man (for example, he may already have been married) or because he may have been a person she did not wish to have identified as her child's progenitor. In some cases, the adoption, mothers were told, would be simplified if the father was unnamed, because it meant that his consent was not required.

These arguments may work for ephemeral relationships between the birth mother and the birth father, but another response is required for the frequent long term relationships that an adoption interrupted (reported separately by Harkness (1991), Nicholls and Levy (1992), Carlini (1993), Clapton (2003) and Witney (2003)). Birth fathers who have maintained strong feelings for the birth mother are unlikely to have forgotten the events surrounding the adoption and the consequences for the child and both birth parents. One might expect these to be the fathers who, even if they did not see their child, would later try to locate the birth mother, to determine her welfare. Yet these men have not, with infrequent exceptions, been forthcoming. Why?

Perhaps there are clues from studies that have focussed not on birth fathers, but other participants, when addressing post-adoption issues. According to Jones, for birth mothers, "Having evaluated the available resources, most concluded that *only* other birthmothers could understand their feelings or problems; many were unable to trust or confide in anyone else" (1993, p140). The implication here is that birth mothers' healing is aided by the empathy of other birth mothers. This need for validation, applied to birth fathers, is reinforced by Gediman and Brown: "In circles where birthfathers feel more or less comfortable, one can hear men admit to feeling 'guilty as hell' that they didn't come through for their [children] or [the birth mothers]" (1991, p183). This last comment is helpful. Whilst birth fathers may feel guilty about not being there for the birth mother and their child, they may be unwilling to share their feelings amongst other birth mothers and adopted persons, people who could judge them harshly. Further, because men often internalise their feelings, a birth father may not be aware that there are other birth fathers who share his responses to loss. He may believe he is an island in a sea of male peer indifference.

Birth fathers are under-represented in studies about the impact of adoption on the members of the family of origin. This is in part a reflection of the general unwillingness of birth fathers to come forward. I suspect that, for several reasons, the majority of birth fathers do not make themselves available in the aftermath of an adoption. Some are unaware of their status. Others prefer to continue to deny that they fathered a child who was adopted. Many feel that they are not ready to explore and share their adoption issues. I believe that these factors conspire to keep a comprehensive birth father view suppressed. Those birth fathers who are represented in published studies typically have addressed, at least to some degree, how they feel about their adoption experiences. I maintain that these men are the fortunate minority.

The traditional societal view of the birth father is that he is the feckless lothario. Other persons with adoption experiences are also members of the community. They may both reflect and contribute to the stereotype that surrounds the birth father.

Adopted persons, in particular, looking for any image of the birth father, may internalise the general view and this can have a negative effect on how they view the man they have never met – they may assume that he fits the popular perception and consider that he is not worth knowing.

In the study by Howarth, which records the stories of adopted persons, I was heartened by the high proportion of searchers who included the birth father in their quest. Howarth relates this to the "many adoptees who believe they have a right to knowledge of their origins, both through contact with their birth mother *and* father, regardless of the circumstances surrounding their conception and birth" (1988, p183) [emphasis in the original]. From an earlier source, written from the perspective of an adopted person who found her birth father after more than forty years of effort, Florence Fisher says, "This was my natural father, and finding him more than justified the unspeakable search that had occupied almost my whole life" (1973, p20).

Regrettably, I have not seen this consideration of the birth father repeated in publications that post-date Howarth. Perhaps the view of one of the adopted persons in her book is still a factor that guides and inhibits some adopted persons. David says he has no desire for contact with his birth father and defends his personal position with: "Why should I? ... fifteen minutes versus nine months" (1988, p93). I consider David's view to be unhelpful. He not only reinforces the stereotype of the birth father as the man who has his sport and moves on, but he also infers that the man is the villain and the birth mother is the victim.

Phillips (2004) presents a contrary viewpoint. She battles her (birth) mother's lack of understanding of her, Zara's, need to know her birth father. Phillips asserts that establishing the father–daughter connection is as important to her as knowing Pat, the mother. "I miss not knowing what he looks like, who he is, what kind of man he is ..." (p126) and "I am sometimes jealous of others who have spent time with their [birth] fathers" (p147).

Overcoming the hurdles

Evidence, supported by the formation of post-adoption support groups specific to their needs, suggests that birth mothers broke through the barriers faced today by birth fathers, more than twenty years ago. A birth mother's guilt may centre on her not having fulfilled the primary mothering role, that of caring for and rearing her child, a significant stigma of neglect for her to overcome in the eyes of the community. Yet birth mothers did and continue to come forward, to share their experiences and achieve a measure of healing.

A birth father's guilt may concentrate on his not fulfilling the traditional male role of the provider/protector. Perhaps the common male reluctance to share feelings and to admit to shortcomings, coupled with guilt, compounded because he has affected the lives of the mother and the child, is a barrier that some birth fathers feel they are unable to surmount. This shield can prevent progress, because it affects not only how these birth fathers feel about themselves, but also their capacity to convey their concerns to others. Often, a birth father's defence may be to deny all feelings about the adoption and its consequences, simply because this strategy seems more manageable and less risky. This reaction is less common amongst birth mothers, who seem to realise that progress is not possible without opening up emotionally, to themselves and to the community. If few men are willing to be transparent about their adoption experiences, then it is not surprising that birth fathers find it difficult to start, let alone maintain support groups. This however, does not imply that birth fathers are condemned to isolation and denial. It does mean that men may have to dedicate time and effort to overcoming the inhibitors that lie largely within themselves.

That men often do not express their feelings is echoed by a newspaper article about men's experiences of in-vitro fertilisation treatment (*The Age,* 3 October 2004). One father involved in the programme comments that "in more than five years' involvement with IVF, he had never heard another man even raise the subject of male infertility, let alone men's feelings." In an echo of the often-heard comment about adoption, IVF is considered to be 'women's business'.

Robinson points out that parents may feel differently about the child they lost to adoption, depending on whether the adopted person is still a minor or has become an adult. Before the adopted child reaches adulthood, "many parents try to persuade themselves that adoption has been best for their children and have difficulty considering any other possibilities" (2004, p12). Whilst their children are minors, birth parents often assume a self-protective mode and any thoughts of searching are deferred. Also, under most jurisdictions, any outreach made by a birth parent to their pre-adult child must by law be directed through the adoptive parents. This is a scenario, in situations where birth and adoptive parents are not in regular contact, that most birth parents avoid, out of consideration for the child, as well as, perhaps, their own emotional fragility.

When both parties are adults, other factors come into consideration. As the child reaches adulthood, the birth parents are typically in the mid-span of their years, often a time when subsequent children they have parented are on the cusp of becoming or have become adults, so consolidating their own identities. This is also a time when parents perhaps contemplate their lives to date. Sometimes, memories of the past may be resurrected by the arrival of grandchildren. Mid-life may be when a birth parent feels that they are ready to search, not only for their authentic self, but also for the now adult child whom they lost through adoption. Also, it may coincide with the time when birth parents are aware that the child they lost is legally now able to initiate the search for their antecedents. Irrespective of who initiates the search, the sought reunion is between two adults, each in a position to take responsibility for their own actions and decisions.

A self-aware birth parent may initiate personal mending as preparation for the possibility of being 'found' by his adult child, albeit as a postponed activity. As noted by Cicchini (1993), for birth fathers, mid-life may represent the time they finally accept responsibility for past actions, including the placement of their child for adoption. Maturity, with accompanying altruism, and the space for reflection may also play a role in the timing. Thus, it may be years, even decades after the event, that birth fathers allow themselves to ponder, as 'men', the full consequences of the actions they took, in many cases, when they were adolescents. This may be the first time the father has faced the hurt he caused the mother, and by association, the child she carried through pregnancy, to lose to an adoption. This may be when he finally admits to and confronts his own pain, the time when he permits his submerged emotional responses to the losses to surface. These feelings may include a postponed reaction to the grief he perhaps suppressed at the time of the adoption. In parallel with or as a result of dealing with his issues, the birth father may feel that he now wants to reach out to the other members of the family of origin. However, he may hold back because of either an unwillingness to intrude upon the lives of the adult child and the birth mother, or negative perceptions about the reception he might receive.

There are good reasons for the delay of a birth father's acknowledgment of the impact of adoption upon himself. Because a birth father does not carry a child for nine months and establish in-utero bonding and because he is often not present at the birth of his child, it may be easier for him to deceive himself that the loss of his child has had little impact on his sense of self. This does not mean that a father ceases to have any regard for his child after the adoption. There is evidence that birth fathers think "frequently" or "constantly" about their child (Cicchini, 1993, p8), whilst at the same time choosing to do nothing about their concerns, until a catalyst for action occurs. For a birth mother, the loss of her child is likely to be an ever-present factor in her life. Because of the severing of the biological bond she forged with her unborn baby, a birth mother is perhaps more likely to have a high degree of continuing awareness of the impact of being separated from her child. However, for birth fathers, in part because of the absence of the biological in-utero linkage, there may be a postponed awareness of the impact of parent–child separation on their lives. A birth mother may rue the lost opportunity to fulfil the traditional role of nurturing her child. A birth father may regret not being there to act as the protector/provider for his family of origin.

When a birth father does decide to confront his adoption experience, he may find that he has significant barriers to overcome, a legacy of both the dual focus of his guilt and the time he has buried his feelings. Birth fathers may bury their guilt for many years, because it feels too confronting to expose their selves to themselves, let alone others. As noted by Jones, the load may be so great that, even within an apparently safe environment, some birth fathers elect to stay 'closed' – "Many [birth mothers married to the birth father] believed that the birthfathers would have preferred to remain in permanent denial rather than risk confrontations with their long-buried emotions" (1993, pp238–239).

Compounded guilt, centred on mother and child, may be the anxiety that either impels a birth father to act out of a sense of remorse or drives him to seek refuge within himself. It may provide either the incentive or an impediment to searching and to healing. A birth father's guilt may be either too much to bear or too much to bare. In the latter circumstance, birth fathers opt to internalise their pain. They may take no action to deal with their past, and so be in a position to assist the birth mother and the now adult child with their recoveries. It is possible that these men have little or no appreciation of the withheld opportunities to help the other members of the family of origin to heal. This insight is likely to arise only after a birth father has dealt with his own adoption issues. The realisation that effort is required may dawn slowly, as occurred in my case. Progress can be faltering, because the perceived risks appear to outweigh the potential benefits of exposure. If he is contacted by his (adult) adopted child or the birth mother, the birth father may be prodded into action.

After I spoke on *Radio National* (Australia), soon after the release of *Ever After: Fathers and the Impact of Adoption*, I was contacted by a birth father from another state. He had been so moved by my story, that he decided, wisely, to pull over to the side of the road to restore his equilibrium. Later, after John (who is in his sixties) and I spoke, he was able to draw upon my experience and encouragement to initiate the search for the daughter who had been born four decades ago and whom he had never seen. Here is a man who required a trigger to confront and deal with his emotional pain, many years after the adoption took place.

Because some men (including birth fathers) find it difficult to process their feelings, even when in their forties, fifties and sixties, they may prefer to restrict their search to seeking information about their now adult child, as well as perhaps the birth mother. For these men, knowing that the persons about whose welfare they care are alive, may be enough. In other words, they have satisfied the desire to know and this may be the degree to which they are prepared to search. To make contact and face the probability of having to confront not only their own feelings but also the emotions of those persons from whom they were separated before or at the time of the adoption may be too difficult for some men to tackle. This scenario could account for the reported phenomenon of men, adopted persons and birth fathers alike, being well represented in post-adoption support organisations' enquiry statistics but under-represented in situations that involve interpersonal communication, such as support groups, conferences, seminars and reunions.

The benefits of being open

I believe that those men who sate their curiosity and proceed no further let down themselves and those from whom they were separated. In my opinion, you display generosity not only to yourself but also to your child and his or her birth mother if you reach out and initiate contact, or if approached first, you accept the overture. By making yourself available, you convey to others that you value them as persons. The alternative of invisibility may suggest that you are selfish and uncaring, a perpetuation of the traditional stereotype of the birth father.

As a birth father, you may believe that determining that your child and the birth mother are alive is a significant act, one that appeases your concerns. In itself, this may be psychologically healthy, but it does not benefit the subjects of your curiosity, for they are unlikely to be aware of your personal quest for solace. It is through a willingness to participate in reunion that a birth father displays not only charity and unselfishness, but also that he truly cares about the persons from whom he was separated by the adoption. By reaching out, the birth father presents himself to the birth mother and his adult child. Each can then consider his offer and avail themselves of the opportunity to include him in their respective recoveries.

For those birth fathers who remain closed, evidence suggests that it is unhealthy, physically and psychologically to live under duress. Suppressing a guilty secret and remaining ever-vigilant to ensure that it is never released is stressful. I maintain that you cannot live a full life, one celebrated by personal well-being and an openness with others, if there is a part of yourself that you are afraid to reveal. Not only do you constrain yourself, but you prevent others from knowing your authentic self. It is my experience that family, friends and strangers appreciate your transparency. In addition, they do not fulfil the fears that you may have about being judged harshly by them for your past indiscretions. In other words, the community may be more understanding than you, perhaps mired in guilt, are prepared to contemplate. This alone, apart from the important health considerations, makes disclosure of your adoption experience beneficial.

There is anecdotal evidence from post-adoption support and services organisations in Australia and New Zealand that birth fathers who initiate contact often do so when they have fulfilled their duty to the children that they have raised in a marriage. Now middle-aged, it is as if they have given themselves 'permission' to search for the now adult child they lost to adoption. According to Jennifer Newbould, manager of ARCS in Western Australia (personal communication, 2004), birth fathers who initiate outreach often proceed slowly – a step at a time, punctuated by lengthy pauses. Few seek counselling, but those who do (and these are birth fathers who rarely have spoken of their adoption experience or their feelings) often find the unburdening very therapeutic. Newbould concludes that those birth fathers who search display great patience and seem not to have high expectations. In my opinion, this may be a manifestation of the guilt that birth fathers can retain – a conflict between the personal need to salve their consciences and a reluctance to remind themselves of the hurt they caused mother and child. Advance, then pause (or even retreat) may seem a safe option. Being found is perhaps a more comfortable alternative and here, according to Newbould, more and more adopted people are today acknowledging that they have birth fathers as well as birth mothers. Newbould makes the observation, that in her experience, the birth fathers approached are particularly receptive, more so in general than the birth mothers who are the subjects of contact. I believe that the attitude of partners can be a critical factor here. A birth father's wife without an adoption experience of her own is perhaps more likely to display tolerance than the husband of a birth mother contacted by her child. In the latter circumstance, some husbands do not appreciate being reminded that they did not marry a virgin.

There may be those birth fathers who, aware of their status, resist facing their adoption issues, because they believe that the activity will disrupt their lives. I contend it is the original separation that has already intruded upon their lives. It is by addressing the impact of the parting that birth fathers incorporate their adoption experience into their lives and so achieve progress.

There are other birth fathers who blame the birth mother for the loss of their child. These are the men who perhaps refuse to accept that they too played a role in the events that led to the adoption. In some cases this censure may represent the projection of a birth father's guilt. I maintain that this stance is a selfish one, which is often at odds with the actual events that took place.

For those men who are surprised many years later to be told that they fathered a child, the news presents an opportunity to welcome a new member into their extended family. The degree to which the birth father accepts his new-found status will depend much upon how he views himself. If he is open to exploring possibilities, this incorporation may be smooth. For other more wary, closed men, this information may be perceived as a threat.

If the claim of paternity from the searching child (now an adult) is well-founded, then a birth father might well pause to consider that his son or daughter has reached out to him, put aside his shock and any apprehensions and honour the initiative taken. Reunion, whether activated by yourself or the other person from whom you were separated prior to or at the time of the adoption, presents an opportunity for reconciliation. If the reunion is perceived to be likely to change the lives of the participants, this is an expected response. In the case of father and child, the meeting presents the first opportunity to experience mirroring (seeing yourself in the other person), allowing issues embracing identity, loss and grief to surface.

Other birth fathers who have no information about their child on which to base a search, may feel relieved to be approached. When Florence Fisher contacts her birth father after a separation of more than four decades, his spontaneous response is "This is the most wonderful moment of my life!" (Fisher, 1973, p256). He explains: "All these years, ... I used to look at children in the street and think, somewhere I have a daughter. Wherever you were, I didn't know who you were, but I always loved you" (Fisher, 1973, p257). Florence Fisher is an example (some would say an inspiration) to those people who encounter difficulties when they search for members of their birth family. Despite facing apparently insuperable difficulties gaining access to information, she refused to give up and eventually found an avenue to her birth father. She personifies the adage that 'where there's a will, there's a way'.

Sometimes, in the reunion between father and child, birth mothers have the opportunity to provide a facilitation role. If the birth father is not named on the birth certificate and their son or daughter asks the mother for the father's name, I maintain that the interests of the child should be paramount. Every adopted person has the right to know both of his or her birth parents. A child inherits genes, traits and medical history from their male and female antecedents. The birth mother and the birth father can each ensure that the adopted person knows the respective halves of their heritage. A birth mother's generosity may help the child to find the birth father, as well as an essential part of his or her identity.

Admitting to fathering a child is not the end of the world. Rather, you may find, as I did, that it represents the launching of a fulfilling phase of your life. You may feel liberated, relieved that the truth is out, that you no longer have to carry the burden of a secret about your past. You may find that you are capable (at last!) of enjoying much of what life has to offer. You will perhaps discover that, as a result of being more open, that the breadth and depth of your friendships increase. Ultimately, of course, you are better prepared to appreciate reunion with the persons from whom you were separated by the adoption, and so give of yourself for their (and your) benefit.

Stromberg comments that to improve how they are perceived by the community, "Birth fathers need ... to portray themselves not as villains, but deserving members of society and of the adoption system. This can be done through the telling of life stories by birth fathers via the media and literature" (2002, p83). Stromberg then makes a telling point – "it is much easier for society to lay blame on a faceless institution rather than an individual and therefore birth fathers ... need to promote an image that contrasts with the traditional image portrayed by society. Birth fathers could then be viewed from a different paradigm" (*ibid*). I urge all birth fathers to rise to this challenge.

SECTION FOUR

Separation and Integration

Transparent

"I will heal me of my grievous wound" – *Alfred, Lord Tennyson*

This trio of essays expands on the central themes of the book. **Separation and Integration** *identifies the emotional consequences of an adoption and highlights the importance of addressing the legacy, so that healing is indeed possible. As a group, the articles embrace all three members of the family of origin – the mother, the father and the child. Never before in adoption literature has the birth father been accorded equal consideration. My landscape is 'closed' adoptions, those arranged around birth and adoptive parents, who were strangers and remain so, unless brought together by the adopted person as an adult.*

This brief piece sets the scene for the two essays that follow. Cause and Effect *describes the assumptions and the presumptions that often accompanied the separation of a child from their birth parents. Drawing upon research, it identifies the actual consequences of the severance.*

1. Cause and effect

In the third quarter of the twentieth century, when the numbers of adoptions peaked, the belief that an adoption benefited the participants and provided a convenient solution for all was accompanied by an expectation that the birth parents, the adopted person and the adoptive parents could continue with their lives as if the separation and placement had never occurred. Rarely, if ever, were the consequences of the splitting of a family of origin discussed before an adoption took place, if indeed they were acknowledged. Advice from parents, social and church workers may have been, on occasions, well meaning, but rarely were their words informed by practical experience. This lack of comprehension did not prevent social workers and others from assuring birth parents that giving up a child was in the mother's, the father's and the child's best interests, at the time and forever.

In particular, there was a presumption that mothers, who had experienced the ignominy of giving birth to a child out of wedlock and been relieved of the evidence, would also be released from an emotional attachment to the child. Some members of the public believed that it was obvious that the mother could not care for her child, otherwise she would have resisted all the advice and kept the baby. In a social setting where illegitimacy was kept a dark secret, mothers (and fathers) who lost their children through adoption were discouraged from ever revealing how they felt about their loss. As a result of these falsehoods and society's condemnation of their 'mistake', many birth parents believed that they were failures, when they found that they could not forget their child.

It took investigations by authors such as Winkler and van Keppel (1984) and Robinson (2003) to overturn these unkind fables, as they applied to birth mothers. These studies revealed that mourning the loss of a child to adoption was to be expected and encouraged, if healing was to occur. Coles (2004) discussed the impact of adoption on birth fathers, identifying the unique qualities of this experience. Likewise, studies by Lifton (1988), Brodzinsky *et al* (1993) and Verrier (1993) revealed the legacy of the original parent–child separation on adopted persons, in particular the breaking of the primal mother–child bond. The overwhelming conclusion of all of this research is that the splitting of the family of origin does not provide the lasting pain-free solution, advocated by many without an adoption experience of their own.

Instead, there have been and continue to be significant issues of well-being for many of those separated by an adoption. Kaplan and Silverstein (1991) highlighted what they called the Seven Core Issues of Adoption, *viz* Loss, Rejection, Guilt/Shame, Grief, Identity, Intimacy and Control, as they apply to adopted persons, birth parents (actually birth mothers) and adoptive parents. For the purposes of alignment and to fill the gap, Coles (2004, pp192–193) applied this model, in which each attribute has an equal weighting, to birth fathers. Thus far, the seven core issues have been described individually. Hitherto, they have not been reviewed for possible linkages and sequencing. In what follows in this section, I have opted for a cause and effect approach, one not explored previously. I believe that this fresh perspective on the results of an adoption is aligned with what members of the family of origin actually experience.

Footnote

In 2004, the Australian Tax Office (ATO) granted Public Benevolent Status to the Adoption Research & Counselling Service (ARCS), of Western Australia. This allows ARCS to claim tax deductibility on any donations received. To win this status, ARCS had to convince the ATO that there is pain and suffering in adoption. They also had to establish that the services they provided alleviated the distress.

Here is official recognition that adoption does cause wounds, which, with appropriate attention and care, can be soothed. For the many who have personal experiences, this ruling is a victory – the twin myths that adoption benefits all participants and leaves no legacies have been overturned.

This is the most comprehensive of the articles in the book. In it, I analyse the impact of the original separation on the birth parents and the child. I describe the facets of the wounding that occur for each member of the family of origin. To prepare for reunion, I advocate that all three persons take personal responsibility for their healing. I expose and extol the benefits of purposeful actions.

2. The long and wounding road

In *Ever After: Fathers and the Impact of Adoption,* I concluded that fundamentally my search was both for my son and my self. I also wrote that, from the perspective of a birth parent, "The basic purpose of searching for the child you were separated from by adoption is to resolve the grief resulting from your loss and so heal the self" (Coles, 2004, p230) and "... reunion represents the opportunity for grief resolution and identity settlement" (p231). As a prelude to the first statement, I noted that, in my opinion, other reasons advanced for searching, such as an abiding curiosity and the expiation of guilt were but symptoms of the grief resulting from the initial loss. Robinson (2004) has expressed similar views in *Adoption and Recovery: Solving the mystery of reunion.* In her book, she explores the two aspects of the parent and the child working to mend the damage caused by the initial separation, which she calls 'personal recovery' and 'interpersonal recovery'. As the terms suggest, the former relates to the self and the latter applies to reunion. Robinson also records the following attributes as components of grief: anger, numbness, sadness, hopelessness, confusion, guilt, depression, and a sense of unreality and fear (Robinson, 2004, Introduction and p51). These investigations provide the ideal framework within which to evaluate the most frequently recorded emotional experiences of an adoption.

I believe that it is unhelpful to consider Kaplan and Silverstein's key issues of Loss, Rejection, Guilt/Shame, Grief, Identity, Intimacy and Control as discrete entities. This approach suggests that they are not interconnected; that one can be considered independently of the others. I believe that it is difficult to argue against a link between loss and grief, with the former the trigger for the latter. Furthermore, who we are and what we think of ourselves (*ie* Identity) is surely related to the impact of the other matters (Rejection, Guilt/Shame, Intimacy and Control) upon us. These patterns suggest start and end points (Loss and Identity) of a fresh approach to evaluating the legacy of an adoption.

I contend that the key issues are best considered as a continuum that begins with the separation, which causes reactions (or wounds) that must be (ad)dressed before recovery is possible. I have depicted this in Figure 1 (Parent and Child – Separation and Integration), which displays the consequences of an adoption. For the sake of simplicity, I have shown the birth parents as an entity, because the emphasis is on the separation of parent and child.

The initial parting results in a loss for the birth parents and their child. For each person, the primary loss may produce a range of grief reactions embracing denial, anger, guilt, shame and diverse fears, which require a resolve (commitment) to take action before recovery is possible. The manifestations of grief are led by denial, because, if this response is rigid, it is unlikely that the individual will be in a position to acknowledge the other facets. The loss also contributes to issues surrounding identity, particularly feelings of self-worth. To mend, the birth parent and the (adult) child undertake a programme of reconciliation and repair. The search is both for their 'whole' selves and the other person. This journey, incorporating the decision to change from being acted upon to taking action, is displayed below.

Figure 1: **Parents and Child — Separation and Integration**

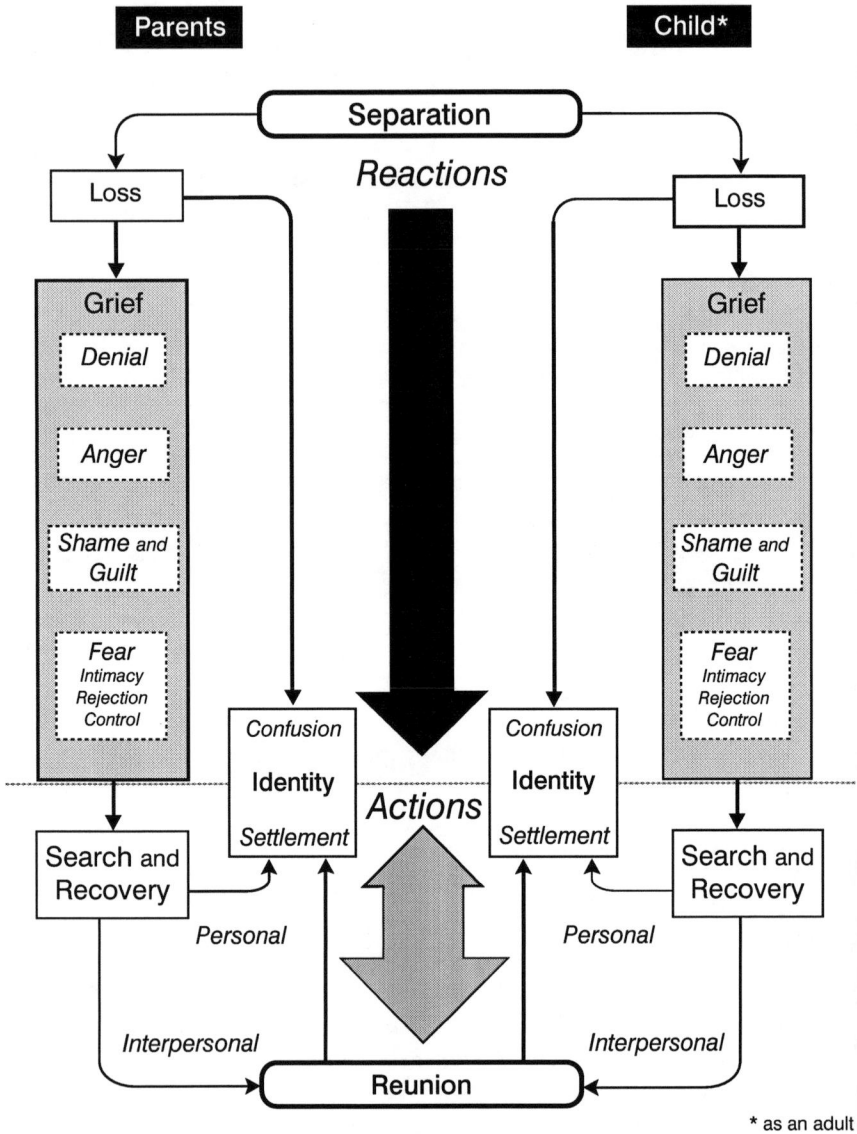

Parents   **Child***

Separation

Reactions

Loss   Loss

Grief   Grief

Denial   *Denial*

Anger   *Anger*

Shame and Guilt   *Shame and Guilt*

Fear
Intimacy
Rejection
Control

Fear
Intimacy
Rejection
Control

Confusion
Identity
Settlement

Confusion
Identity
Settlement

Actions

Search and Recovery   Search and Recovery

Personal   *Personal*

Interpersonal   *Interpersonal*

Reunion

* as an adult

Some people affected by adoption separation may choose not to explore the legacy. Perhaps they contend that the loss and the grief reactions they feel are unexceptional. Some may eschew the possibility of taking actions to understand and address the impact of family separation, because they believe that to do so could threaten their equilibrium. Such people often deny the impact of adoption upon their lives and remain stuck in the separation phase. They do not display a willingness to explore why they feel as they do. Other people choose to challenge the status quo and to take action to comprehend and address their reactions. They opt to pursue search and recovery. In my opinion, it is these people, intent upon integrating their adoption experiences into their lives, who provide themselves with the opportunity to achieve personal growth. Such persons acknowledge that an awareness of cause and effect is integral to their understanding of the consequences of separation, and achieving integration. In what follows, I examine each phase of the continuum.

Loss

Frequently references in adoption literature to birth parents are, in fact, to the mother only. It is as if the father does not exist. Consequently, studies of the impact of separation on the family of origin have tended to focus on the birth mother and the adopted person.

However, when there is an adoption, a family disintegrates. A child is removed from <u>both</u> their birth parents and losses occur. The birth parents lose the child to whom they are genetically connected. They lose the opportunity to raise the child, to fulfil the traditional parenting role. The birth mother and the birth father may also lose one another, if, prior to the adoption, they enjoyed a meaningful relationship. (Interpersonal matters for birth parents are explored in the next essay.)

Adopted persons lose their birth parents, family ties with blood relatives (including siblings), genealogical continuity and everyday evidence of their heritage. The bond between mother and child is broken when the child is placed with adoptive parents, who offer a less fundamental connection. This is expressed neatly by Sally Howard, who notes that "In families kept intact, bonding happens and so does attachment. In [adoptive families] this is not the case because there can only be an attachment" (2003, p127). An adopted person may not remember the original separation cognitively, but experience at a deeper level what Verrier calls "an aching sense of loss ... about which there are no conscious thoughts, only feelings and somatic memories" (1993, p27). Howard likens the separation from her birth mother to an amputation (2003, p127). In the aftermath of the separation from their birth parents, adopted persons suffer another loss – the absence of a biological connection with their adoptive parents.

Brodzinsky *et al* (1993, pp74–76) compare the three common causes of loss in childhood – death, divorce and adoption. Whilst there are many similarities, there are also significant differences. With death, the departed person cannot return. After a divorce, the separated parent and child often maintain contact. In the case of a closed adoption, an adopted person and their birth parents are estranged, but the loss retains an unclosed quality. The adopted person may fantasise that the situation is reversible, for the birth parents are still alive. For the same reason, birth parents may contemplate the re-appearance of their child. Because an adopted person has no history of a relationship with the birth parents, the birth mother and the birth father often linger as ghosts, making the loss difficult to rationalise. At the core, an adopted person has lost two birth parents and the heritage they provide, as well as genetic connections with grandparents, siblings, aunts and uncles and cousins. By losing their genealogical and cultural linkages, they have also lost a part of themselves. Because the loss is rarely recognised by the community, there are few rituals or support systems in place to help the child deal with the consequences of the initial separation.

Two weeks after the December 2004 tsunamis devastated the coastal regions of several countries bordering the Indian Ocean, an article about loss appeared in *The Age*. The writer, Peter Ellingsen, highlights the difficulties friends and relatives experience dealing with the unknown. "It produces an awful emptiness. There's a possibility of finding him alive, or dead, or not at all," says one of the persons affected. This quotation mirrors what a member of a birth family might say. Ellingsen concludes that in the situation described, this response is to be anticipated: "... loss is what is perceived, not what in fact happens." A missing person "can trigger all the instinctive behaviours associated with grieving."

Verrier discusses the two ways in which an adopted person typically deals with loss. She characterises the behaviour of the acting-out child as a distancing in an "externalised, overt, provocative manner", whilst the compliant child deals with his recurring fear of abandonment by "distancing in an internalized, withdrawn, acquiescent manner" (2003, p154). As Verrier (1993) points out, these are strategies to cope with the initial loss and the potential for further losses. Neither person is exhibiting his true grieving personality for fear that if this was exhibited, it might not be appreciated by himself or significant others.

For birth mothers, van Keppel *et al* (1987, p4) record that their "sense of loss is typically strong and long-lasting", an observation that parallels a finding of the 1984 study by Winkler and van Keppel, which showed that approximately 50 per cent of a group of birth mothers studied reported an increase in their feelings of loss over time. Van Keppel *et al* also remind us that losing a child to adoption is accompanied by, for the birth mother, other losses, such as support, self-esteem, income and independence. As noted by van Keppel *et al*, "relinquishing a child for adoption was the most stressful life-event birth mothers had ever experienced" (1987, p3).

Clapton reports a similar finding for the birth fathers that he studied. "For many the adoption and loss of their child was a milestone or 'peak' on a graph of the emotional and psychological geography of their lives" (2003, p151). Some birth fathers may experience this as a delayed reaction emotionally, because perhaps it was their rational, practical selves that dealt with the crisis that culminated in the adoption of their child. Celia Witney (personal communication, 2003), in her study of sixty men, noted a three way loss for birth fathers – of their child, their lover and self-esteem. One birth father in Cicchini's Australian study voiced an echo of what birth mothers have found – "The feelings of loss, emptiness and helplessness have increased with every passing year" (1993, p16). Birth father Steve Davis reports in Lowe (undated) that he has "learned to live with a lot of pain and regret. Adoption isn't something that just happens and then you get on with your life. It's permanent, and it affects your life forever." Another birth father comments: "We carry these ghosts of our children in our hearts forever" (Stallings, 2004, p14). Neglecting to fulfil the traditional male protector/provider role may be a component of the loss that birth fathers experience.

Jones (1993) observes, based on her canvassing of the views of seventy-two birth mothers, that in the aftermath of giving up a child to adoption, the women struggled emotionally with "rage, frustration, sorrow, guilt, and self-doubt" (p7). Jones amplifies this conclusion: "Whether they'd been active or passive in the decision-making process ... all had experienced losses that they needed to address. For some, the need focussed completely on the loss of their babies. For others, it was more diffuse, including intangible losses such as the role of mother, self-esteem, or the sense of being 'good' or even 'normal' " (1993, p73). Because of the in-utero bond forged in pregnancy, a mother does not forget her child.

Grief

Grief is usually associated with the loss of another, but is always personal. When Mark Dent loses a limb to bone cancer, he reports that "The amputation of my leg was a terrible loss. I still grieve deeply for my faithful right leg" (1997, p96).

According to Brodzinsky *et al*, "Grieving almost always follows loss. It has many emotional and behavioral manifestations: shock, anger, depression, despair, helplessness, hopelessness. Grief can be blocked or it can be prolonged, but usually it is a normal and adaptive response to the experience of loss" (1993, p11).

Evelyn Robinson provides an adoption setting for the conjunction between loss and grief. "You cannot have adoption without loss. Grief is not only the *expected* response to a loss, but it is also a **positive and beneficial** response, because grieving allows us to process our loss" (2001b, p2) [emphases in the reference]. The cause and effect connections are clear. An adoption results in loss, of which grief is the anticipated outcome.

Russell provides a grief framework for those with adoption experiences. "Grieving in adoption is different in some distinct ways from mourning the death of someone who has died. When someone dies, there is a definite ending that allows the grieving to begin. In adoption, there is no death, no ending. In adoption, a state of limbo exists that is similar to the dynamics of mourning someone who is missing in action. Not knowing where the person is or if they are alive blocks the grieving process. It is difficult to mourn someone who is alive but unavailable" (1996, pp46–47).

As Robinson (2003) identifies, there are often other, externally imposed impediments to grieving, which are embraced by the term 'disenfranchisement'. Disenfranchised grief translates into the relationship, the loss and the griever all not being recognised by the community. As Robinson (2002) points out, "the grief of mothers who have lost children in this way is usually suppressed. Many mothers state that they did not feel that they were entitled to grieve the loss of their children ... there were no rituals and there was no gathering of the community to comfort them at the time of separation from their children" (p58). In the same article, about post-adoption grief counselling for birth mothers, Robinson acknowledges that "a number of women had been led to believe that grieving for the loss of their child was itself a sign of inadequacy on their part, making them reluctant to admit to their ongoing pain" (*ibid*). This, Robinson (2001a) observes, has consequences for birth mothers. "They usually have difficulty dealing with subsequent losses, because they did not learn how to grieve productively in what for most of them was the first major loss in their lives ..." (p3). In the case of adoption, there seems to be a clear linkage between 'unfinished business' and grief.

Clapton concludes that the thirty birth fathers in his study reported suffering "feelings, behaviours and experiences" that had "parallels with what birth mothers may go through: a pathological grief reaction born of a sense of loss" (2003, p119). He reinforces how the loss is different from a typical bereavement: "In adoption the child is 'lost' yet lives on", an experience without a point of reference in the community. Clapton highlights further similarities with the reactions of birth mothers – the feelings of distress and powerlessness, as well as the persistence of the feelings of grief over a long period (2003, p119 and p206).

For adopted persons, Verrier observes, the grief experienced by a child who is separated from his birth mother has seldom been acknowledged. "It has been assumed that any deprivation which might have occurred could be overcome by the adoptive parents" (1993, p39). However, according to Robinson,

> "... in recent years has come the realisation that adopted people, regardless of how apparently problem-free their adoptions have been, experience a deep and painful sense of loss because they have been separated from their natural mothers. Their grief resulting from this loss is not always obvious because it has usually been suppressed and is often exhibited indirectly in the behaviour of adopted people,

especially in the adolescent years ... Adopted people, like their natural mothers, have not been encouraged by society to express their grief, as the expectation was that they would be grateful to their adoptive parents for 'rescuing' them. Society has traditionally admired adoptive parents for doing what appeared to be a community service by adopting children who were thought to be without families. In fact, these children did have families and they suffered from having spent their lives separated from them" (2003, pp112–113).

Robinson then draws parallels between the disenfranchised grief experienced by adopted persons and their mothers.

"Adopted people, like natural mothers, lack a concrete focus for their grief, as they usually have no conscious memory of their natural mothers. There is also no finality to their grief, as they know that they have other families somewhere and that they will always, in some way, be a part of these families. Adopted people lack any rituals to facilitate their grieving, as they were not intellectually aware at the time that the adoption took place ... Like their natural mothers, they have often not expressed their true feelings of loss and so too often the assumption has been made that those feelings did not exist. As their natural mothers appeared to 'get on with their lives' and often showed no outward signs of their inner turmoil, so adopted people often appear to be content with their lot and show no obvious signs of grieving" (2003, p114).

Robinson concludes that adopted people "grieve for the loss of their mothers and their natural families and that this grief affects their feelings of self-worth ..." (2003, p122).

When Zara Phillips meets her birth mother, she realises through her pain that the loss of her primary caregiver has left a legacy of unresolved grief (2004, p88). Griffith asserts that unresolved grief is at the core of the many tensions that adopted persons experience, which social workers and others find difficult to penetrate – "I believe the high degree of frustration often experienced in getting adopted persons to fully work through key issues such as rejection, anger, suppression of feelings, denial and identity conflicts, is often the failure to recognise the underlying grief" (personal communication, 2004). Griffith's observation is a further acknowledgment of the spectrum of grief manifestations.

Dent (1997) is a person without an adoption experience, who can provide guidance for those suffering from grief. Noting a propensity for the public to assume that a person who displays sorrow many years after experiencing a loss "has stopped living, creating and looking forward in their own life" (p115), he asserts, that to the contrary, he is living a full life, facilitated by a commitment to continue to process the loss of his leg. "I will never ignore my grief. I will never belittle or trivialise my feelings. If I feel deep hurt, I will acknowledge it, knowing that it will pass for a time but also aware that it will return, perhaps less painfully, some time in the future ... I refuse to bottle up the [emotional] pain – that is pointless ..." (Dent, 1997, p99).

In Figure 1, I have acknowledged that grief is the fundamental manifestation of loss. Individuals express their grief in various ways. Beyond profound sorrow, grieving behaviours include denial, anger, guilt, shame and various fears. Each is explored below.

Denial

Denial is the defensive mechanism applied to avoid confronting unpleasant facts. It may be used to block the processing of grief and become an impediment to the employment of anger to bring about change. It may be a barrier to the acknowledgment of guilt and reinforce the fear of intimacy and/or rejection. Denial represents a reluctance to face the truth, and is thus the most debilitating of the grief reactions, because it represents avoidance and a stationary position. If feelings are suppressed deliberately, then the scope for the affected individual to recognise the multiple consequences of loss is severely compromised.

Verrier notes that the state of what she calls 'numbing' is characterised for adopted persons by "emotional detachment, indifference, complacency, and passivity" (1993, p72). According to Russell, "Many adoptees would be too overwhelmed by the reality of their situation if they experienced clarity. Instead, living with fogginess feels comforting and protective. To have clarity is a challenge for many people. For adoptees, certain feelings may be too intense to confront" (1996, p75).

For me, as a birth father, this was so for 25 years. My denial manifested itself with a lack of willingness to confront my role in the placement of my son for adoption. The fortress I had constructed about myself did however have a few cracks, for I experienced bouts of anger directed against objects (not people), accompanied by a guilt that, in the past, I had wronged persons I cared about. This feeling was deep and hazy, because I refused to allow it substance and exposure. Likewise, birth father Jim Shinn recalls that after the adoption of his son, "I entered into a period of a lot of denial" (Blau, 1993, p124).

Jones (1993) reports that after the loss of their child, "Many birthmothers ... completely banished their feelings and unwittingly blocked themselves from completing the grieving process. By burying rather than experiencing their anger and [sorrow], they became stuck in denial" (p81). Jones notes further that many birth mothers internalised the judgments of their families and society. One mother, Alexis, unable to acknowledge her feelings of loss, instead dismissed them, because, at first she believed them to be 'wrong' and later because she had begun to deny them altogether (pp79–80). "Eventually, despite her deliberate suppression and conscious denial of her feelings, Alexis became debilitated by inexplicable bouts of depression and anger" (p80). I suggest that in this quotation, 'despite' could be replaced by 'because of', to reflect an actual cause and effect connection.

Anger

This reaction is not one of the Seven Core Issues identified by Kaplan and Silverstein. However, often it is recorded as a consequence of adoption and loss, and on this basis, I believe that it deserves to be included.

The emotion of anger, used wisely, can protect us from hurt and exploitation. However, if misused, it is no longer an ally, but a problem and a hindrance. According to Russell "Anger is an emotion that naturally occurs when there is a loss or a feeling of being out of control. Anger can also motivate people to actions such as searching for their child or fighting for adoption reform" (1996, p85).

Evelyn Robinson, in an article entitled *Some thoughts on anger*, relates her personal experience.

> "I spent my pregnancy being angry that I suddenly had this huge responsibility to deal with on my own. I was angry at all the people who turned their backs on me but I was also angry with all the people who thought they were being helpful because I knew that actually none of them could help me. Most of all I was angry on behalf of my child because he was not welcomed into the world with joy the way he should have been; and after my child was gone I was angry with myself for letting him go. Over the years as I thought about him growing up, I was angry at his adoptive parents because they were sharing his childhood and his development and I was not. I was angry too that while many had encouraged me to give him up for adoption, now there were also many people making me feel ashamed of my decision" (2000a, p10)

To help others, Robinson then puts her anger into context.

> "The important thing to realise is, that if you feel this way too, it's not surprising and it's nothing to apologise for ... It would be very strange if we didn't feel this rage and it would be unhealthy for us to repress it. We need to be careful,

however, what we do with it ... It's natural for us to feel anger and it's fine to express our anger in a safe environment ... It's not fine, in my opinion, for us to direct our anger towards others, who were, like us, acting the way society expected them to act. We were all taken in by the myths that existed at the time; not only us but also our parents, our social workers and our children's adoptive parents" (2000a, pp10–11).

Robinson advocates that we process our anger, so that "When we begin to understand why we behaved the way we did and why those other people behaved the way they did, we may find that our anger has already subsided to some degree. We may find that we have then a sense of energy rather than rage and a desire to spread enlightenment and teach the community about our experiences" (2000a, p11). Robinson summarises her views, *viz* "Anger can be a positive and productive emotion. Bitterness is negative and destructive" (2001a, p1). Mary Murray (2002) describes how her initial (productive) reaction of anger precipitated the search for her son, a reinforcement of the benefits of the positive approach.

Verrier warns us that if anger "is inappropriate, it will stimulate aggression, which is an attempt to control or intimidate others. Or it can lead to passivity, which is another form of control, controlling by what one *doesn't* do" (1993, p192) [emphasis in the original].

Lifton notes that for adopted persons, there may be "the unexpressed anger that they are adopted; anger that they are different; anger that they are powerless to know their origins; anger that they cannot express their real feelings in a family climate of denial" (1994, p90). An adopted person may be angry at the birth parents, particularly the primary caregiver, his mother, for, he believes, giving him away. He may also be angry at the adoptive parents for replacing the birth parents. Zara Phillips feels anger towards both her birth mother and her adoptive parents, people who "had planned my future without consulting me" (2004, p63). An adopted person may be angry about the legislation or towards his adoptive parents, for preventing him from finding out about his antecedents.

Verrier concludes that "adopted persons often turn their rage at the unspeakable thing that happened to them on their [adoptive parents]. Although some reunited adopted persons speak of feeling rage for their birth mothers or for the society which caused their separation from her, many will say that they feel no ill-will toward her, but have all their lives exhibited oppositional behaviour and intense rage toward their adoptive parents. Paradoxically, they feel a tremendous dependency upon and need to connect to those same adoptive parents" (1993, pp72–73).

Brodzinsky *et al* (1993, pp156–157) provide another example where anger may surface – the belated revelation in an adoptive family, often when the adopted person is a mature adult, that she is not genetically linked to the persons who raised her. Here the anger may be compounded by the years of information suppression and in some cases, deliberate lies. The anger that these adopted persons feel is often not about the circumstances of their conception and the family arrangements made on their behalf, but rather the withholding of vital information by the parents who have raised them.

I believe that the anger experienced by birth parents and adopted persons can be addressed productively. Through exploring the circumstances of the adoption, in the context of the then prevailing social environment, birth parents may fathom the actions taken by others on their behalf, against a background of community ignorance. For an adopted person, his exploration of the setting in which the adoption took place may assist him to divert his venom away from the birth parents or the adoptive parents and instead focus his misgivings more productively upon comprehending society's attitudes at the time of his placement.

Guilt and Shame

Guilt and shame are sometimes used interchangeably. However, as several writers have pointed out, there is a fundamental difference between the two. Schooler records that "[He] feels guilty for something he has done, and he feels shame for being the type of person who would have done it" (1995, p20).

Verrier reinforces the distinction in this way: "We feel guilty for what we did or imagined that we did; we feel shameful for who we are. It is the difference between *doing* and *being*" (1993, p191) [emphasis in the original]. She continues: "Shame serves no useful purpose because it cannot be integrated. It tells us that we are not worthy. It lowers our self-esteem and sabotages our sense of Self" (*ibid*). Shame is related to how we feel about ourselves; it is linked to our identity. According to Verrier, shame "is the judgment or belief that many adoptees have about themselves because they were given up for adoption" (*ibid*). This may manifest itself in a belief that they were deficient and not worthy of keeping. Verrier goes on: "If a birth mother feels shame, it is probably from some early belief about herself, not because of the relinquishment. Relinquishment is an act, which may lead to guilt" (*ibid*).

Verrier explores the nature of guilt. Asserting that it is a "judgment against ourselves", she concludes that guilt "comes in two varieties. Justifiable guilt is what one experiences when one has harmed another person or engaged in unethical conduct ... When that happens we can make amends and try to avoid repeating the offense ... Neurotic guilt, on the other hand, is guilt about something over which we had no control. It leads to blame, not accountability" (1993, pp190–191). With justifiable guilt, restitution is possible; its admission can be integrated into our lives. Neurotic guilt, however causes conflict and confusion and cannot be resolved. It is often "a cover-up for other feelings such as sorrow or anger" (Verrier, 1993, p191).

Schooler evaluates what shame and guilt mean for an adopted person. Within an adoptive family, a "source of shame for many adopted adults is the feeling that they never were what their adoptive parents had hoped for. They never measured up to the child their parents could not conceive" (1995, p19). Guilt, however, is rooted "in feeling that even as a small child she or he caused the break-up of the relationship within the birth family" (*ibid*). When a female adopted person becomes a mother herself, she may feel, as did Zara Phillips, "guilty for being able to have a baby so easily", because her adoptive mother "had never been able to have the experience of her own child" (2004, p123).

For birth parents, guilt may be the most potent representation of grief and as a result, the most difficult to address. Russell notes that for a birth mother, there "can be guilt about having sex, guilt about getting pregnant, and guilt about deciding on adoption" (1996, p84). There is also the shame and the guilt associated with pleasing others. Birth mother Amy in Jones (1993) explains: "I felt it was wrong to be pregnant and even worse to be sad about it ... I tried to ... act 'normal' to please my parents ... I was ashamed both that I was pregnant and that I *wanted* to be. I'd always been a 'good girl' and I needed to feel that I deserved that title again. But to be a 'good girl' again, my parents said I'd have to do the 'right' thing and give up my baby" (pp18–19) [emphasis in the reference]. For many birth mothers this raises the eternal core dilemma – how could relinquishment be considered both a noble sacrifice and an unmotherly act, for what 'real mother' would give up her child, despite the pressure applied to her to do so? Jones also notes that after they lost their children to adoption many birth mothers, without the support of families and others, "saw themselves as 'bad', 'undeserving of love', 'not worthy' of raising their own children ... for shaming their families, and, most of all, for relinquishing their babies" (1993, p98). Sometimes, for those who influenced the birth mother to give up her child, the guilt may surface decades later, as discovered by Sue (referring to her mother) in Jones, *viz*: "She has felt guilty, all these years, about making me surrender [my son]" (1993, p257). Pace (2004b), referring to the ingrained shame of 'unwed' motherhood, comments about how difficult this burden is to put aside. "Few of us were allowed by parents or circumstances the choice of raising our children. Yet we were stereotyped as those very few mothers who might not have wanted their children, and who abandoned them."

Cicchini (1993), in his analysis of the experiences of thirty Australian birth fathers, concluded that 67% of the men studied felt guilty about the relinquishment of their child (p12) and that a similar number (61%) had felt a need to assuage that guilt by searching for their now adult child (p19). One of the birth fathers in Cicchini's study remarks: "I've carried a lot of guilt and shame about [the relinquishment of my child], and a fear of ... being found out by other people" (1993, p12). Another highlights the frequently mentioned shame-based dilemma for birth parents, when he says, "I don't tell people I have fathered three children (one adopted)" (p13). For some birth fathers, their guilt centres on having let the birth mother down and so leaving her with little choice but to place the child for adoption. "The men associated ... feelings of guilt with having not 'stood up' for themselves (and for the birth mother and the child), with not having done enough to prevent the adoption and, for those who agreed with the adoption (with hindsight perhaps) a belief that they had done something wrong" (Clapton, 2003, p137). Mason (1995) observes that disempowerment and feelings of emotional and physical disconnectedness may trigger feelings of shame or failure; birth fathers can retain images of what could (or should) have been.

It might be assumed that birth fathers who did not know of their paternity would be spared the burden of guilt. However, there is experiential evidence that birth fathers who are informed of their paternity many years after the event, begin, in some cases from the moment of revelation, to feel guilty about the prolonged absence from their child's life.

Fear

There are a number of reactions to loss that I have gathered under the heading of 'Fear'. Each represents at best an anxiety, at worst a dread. Because the fears of intimacy or being rejected or controlled by others have relationships at their core, they may take considerable courage and effort to overcome.

Intimacy

The fear of intimacy relates to trying to avoid the risk of suffering another loss, one that provides a potent reminder of the original parent–child separation. Birth parents and adopted persons alike report that the intimacy which culminated in an adoption often leaves a legacy of distrust and impaired self-esteem.

Kaplan and Silverstein conclude that "people who have had significant losses in their lives may fear getting close to others because of the risk of experiencing loss again" (1991, Section 2, p3). They continue: "Birthparents may connect the loss of their child with the sexual encounter that led to the pregnancy, and fear intimacy because they believe it leads to loss" (*ibid*).

Jones (1993) reports that many of the women in her study felt that their ability to relate to others was compromised after they were separated from their children. "Most agreed that their problems with intimacy were not limited to marriages or relationships with men but extended to friendships with women and interactions with their parents and siblings as well ... Those whose trust and self-confidence had been casualties of relinquishing felt that, without these qualities, their subsequent relationships were, from the start, destined to be impaired" (p139). Sue, one of the women interviewed by Jones, convinced herself that love had been the root cause of her post-relinquishment despair. "As a result, I became afraid of my sexuality ... I became frigid towards men" (p92). Jones also reports that nine out of ten women she interviewed on this topic married within two years of losing their child to adoption. A significant number thought that they had married for the wrong reasons or married the wrong man. For some, social acceptability to escape the stigma of losing a child was the incentive to marry soon after the adoption was finalised. Often, these marriages were loveless, which, as Jones points out, "seemed the most plausible and effective defense against the potential pain of intimacy" (1993, p120). Some birth mothers feel so threatened by the risks of close relationships that they isolate themselves from other people for months, even years, choosing in some cases, never to marry, or to pursue an alternative commitment to a career. Among those who consciously avoided men because "intimacy would only mean further pain ... some went out of their way to avoid attracting the opposite sex" (Jones, 1993, p134).

These sentiments are to some degree echoed by birth fathers. Men in Cicchini's 1993 study report that: "I just can't start a good relationship with a woman. As soon as they get too close I walk away" (p12), "I am finding difficulty forming a lasting meaningful relationship" (p13) and "I drifted from one 'permanent' relationship to the next" (p9). One of the men in Clapton's study of birth fathers concludes that his failure to commit to a partner is affected by caution, which is related to his negative experience of adoption (2003, p145). "Others believed that the adoption experience had influenced their general attitude to all relationships" and "their negative attitudes originated in the experience of loss and disenfranchisement during the adoption" (Clapton, 2003, p147).

According to Verrier (1993), "Many adoptees find it difficult to attach or allow closeness in relationships because of the fear that each new relationship, *like the very first relationship*, will not last" (p90) [emphasis in the original]. Because of this same fear, "Separating seems an even greater problem than attaching. Once a relationship is established many adoptees do not want to separate, even when the relationship proves unsatisfactory" (*ibid*). Simultaneous conflicting desires for merger and independence can create relationship complications for some adopted persons. "The fear of abandonment often keeps an adoptee from getting close to those with whom he is in relationship. When he begins to feel connected to another person, he will do something to distance himself from his partner and find a sense of safety again" (Verrier, 2003, p217). Lifton points out that, for adopted persons who have constructed protective mechanisms to disguise their real feelings, they "often avoid intimacy for fear of being discovered for the impostors they know they are. Let down your guard, they think, and everyone will see that under the confident self you present to the world, there is really a weak and frightened child. Better to keep your distance to avoid being abandoned again" (1994, p115).

Rejection

The fear of rejection is related to our feelings of self-worth. More so than the other fears, rejection may be an unfounded perception and, as such, have the potential to cause the greatest harm, if not assessed objectively. Rejection is our projection of how we fear others may react to us.

Kaplan and Silverstein maintain that "Adoptees often feel they were placed for adoption because they were worthless or defective ... Some may take responsibility for being rejected, believing they did something to cause it" (1991, Section 2, p1). Some link the adoption to the assumption that to be available for their adoptive parents, they had first to be 'given up' by their birth parents.

Russell points out that "Some adoptees protect themselves from the threat of rejection ... by rejecting others before they can be rejected ... For [some] adoptees, the fear of ... rejection is never far away and can interfere with getting close to people" (1996, p69). Schooler concurs, by saying of adopted persons that "Their perceptions of rejection can spill over to affect the building of healthy relationships" (1995, p18). On the same theme Kaplan and Silverstein observe that "Not only can feelings of rejection lead to impaired self-esteem [but] adoptees may anticipate rejection and either set themselves up for it in their relationships or try to please others so they are not rejected" (1991, Section 2, p2). Verrier (2003, p56) explores the impact of these perceptions, by noting that the propensity of many adopted persons to interpret observations as personal criticisms and disagreements with their viewpoint as rejection. These can be personal 'landmines' for adopted persons. Verrier discusses the eternal dilemma for adopted persons. "If someone rejects the outside you, that's not so bad, because it isn't really you; but if you let someone know who you really are inside and they reject you, that's *really* rejection. The 'false' self is the adoptees' method of adjusting to their environment in order to protect themselves from further ... rejection" (1993, p35) [emphasis in the original]. Verrier observes that, in adulthood, adoptees are like chameleons. "They are very good at adapting, because they spent their childhood perfecting the art of adapting to their adoptive families", so avoiding being rejected by their caregivers (2003, p50).

For an adopted person, the fear of rejection may be linked to the original separation. At the time, the infant may internalise the original separation as an abandonment, for the fundamental mother–child bond was broken. An adopted person, as a child, an adolescent and an adult may prepare and use strategies that externalise their fear of rejection by others. Phillips observes: "I didn't want to hurt my [adoptive] mother by asking too many questions, so I began to protect my family from my real feelings ... I didn't want to be rejected" (2004, p22).

Of birth parents, Kaplan and Silverstein comment, "[they] may reject themselves as irresponsible or unworthy to be a parent. They often keep the fact that they placed a child for adoption a secret because they fear people would reject them if they knew the truth" (1991, Section 2, p2). With the benefit of hindsight, one of the birth fathers in Cicchini's study states "Now I would keep the child, not care whether I was rejected by my family or not" (1993, p11).

Post-separation, birth parents can fear rejection by their son or daughter because they may believe that the child will never forgive his mother and father for giving him away. An adopted person may fear that their birth parents will reject them a second time. For those birth parents who have not told their spouse, siblings, later children or parents of the presence of an adopted child, there is the spectre of rejection, should they reveal the secret after an interval of many years. Other birth mothers and birth fathers may have to re-write the script and correct the misinformation they had offered previously. Because of this turnaround, they may fear renunciation.

As a consequence of an adoption, birth parents will perhaps have rejected a part of their selves. This may be manifested by feelings of shame, guilt and worthlessness surrounding the momentous event. For birth parents and adopted persons, the feelings of rejection are often internalised as an element of their self-esteem.

Control

As humans, we prefer to exercise control over our lives, rather than have others impose their will upon us. Often, those people with adoption experiences speak of being disempowered, of having decisions made for them rather than by them. The original parent–child separation is the critical moment for the birth mother, the birth father and their son or daughter. The adoption may leave a legacy of wariness for all members of the family of origin and a resolve to avoid manipulation by others, thereafter.

According to Verrier, "One of the ways in which children (and adults, too) try to prevent future losses is to try to be in absolute control of every situation" (1993, p78). For adopted persons the fear of not being in control is paramount. "*The child was not in control of the situation at the beginning of his life, and look what happened!* It becomes intolerable to these children ever again to allow anyone else to be in control of their lives" (Verrier, 1993, p79) [emphasis in the original]. Many adopted persons develop strategies to maintain control. "Having been manipulated at the beginning of their lives makes some adoptees manipulative and controlling ... Some adoptees control situations by becoming isolated and detached, while others are more overt in their controlling mechanisms" (Verrier, 1993, p97). In her second book, Verrier cautions adopted persons. "Even as you ensure that you are not being controlled by that other person, *you are not in control* ... You are being controlled instead by your own fear of being controlled – by the little scared child inside, who is still in the grips of the fear of that first loss" (2003, p201) [emphasis in the original].

Jones (1993) observes that "No mother in the world, human or animal, would *decide* to give up her baby. It isn't normal or natural. It wouldn't happen if mothers had the power to decide [*ie* be in control]. It only happens when they don't" (p12) [emphasis in the reference]. She records that of the birth mothers interviewed in her study, "most ... relinquished not because they wanted to, but because their pregnancies broke the rules, opposed social standards, and threatened to leave them forever isolated from respectable society" (p13). In the aftermath of the adoption, "Birthmothers ... often began patterns of strict emotional control that they maintained for years ... [They] tried to control their relationships ... Having lacked control over their babies, they were determined to maintain tight reins over the remainder of their lives, often defying authority or rejecting both people and opportunities that represented risk" (Jones, 1993, p99). These women systematically avoided situations in which they again might feel powerless.

Disempowerment is a common reaction reported by birth fathers. The relinquishment of control before and at the time of the birth of their child, frequently to one or both sets of parents, may leave the men feeling that they have failed to fulfil the male role of protector/provider to the birth mother and their child. There is evidence that some birth fathers have over-compensated in subsequent relationships for the control they forsook when their child was adopted.

A few thoughts about Trust

I have not accorded trust the status of a separate entity, principally because its effects are diverse.

Trust is the glue that holds relationships together. For an adopted person, trust may be destroyed by the original mother–child separation. According to PARC, if a mother is "consistent, loving and responsive" in meeting the needs of her baby, then the infant comes to trust her, and attachment develops (2004, p7). Having lost her birth mother, "every adopted child comes to her new family with attachment problems" (*ibid*). As described by Verrier, "The loss of the mother disallows the achievement of basic trust, the first milestone in the healthy development of a human being" (1993, p36). The development of trust is an essential component of identity. It allows adopted (and all) persons to believe in themselves and in others. Trust may affect intimacy; without it, lasting, loving relationships are not possible. Verrier summarises the negative impacts. "Distrust is evident, not only in the permanency of relationships, but in the goodness of self ... This lack of self-esteem or self-worth is intricately intertwined with the lack of trust and fear of intimacy described by many ... adoptees" (1993, p90).

"Many birth mothers," writes Verrier, "have lost their trust in family and professionals. From the time that their family members urged them to give up their babies for adoption, they began to distrust those relationships ... They lost trust, not only in their family members and professionals, but in their own judgment" (2003, p224). According to Jones (1993), when birth mothers confronted the loss of their child, they often encountered issues of broken trust, related to the birth father, family and adoption professionals (p40). For some, the reluctance to trust extended to themselves; "they didn't trust themselves to accomplish, maintain or merit *any* goal or relationship ... Accomplishments in careers, parenting, or other efforts ... were credited to others than themselves" (p125) [emphasis in the original]. Here, the inability to have faith in themselves and to acknowledge personal achievements is rooted in feelings of self-worth, an element of identity.

Identity

Because it has at its heart what we think of ourselves, identity is a bridge that spans separation and healing. It governs how we react to loss and it affects the degree to which we recover from that misfortune.

For an adopted person, the separation of birth parent and child may result in bewilderment about their heritage. Birth parents may feel uncertain about what it means to be a mother or a father. These are issues related to how people view themselves. During the integration phase, awareness, self-responsibility and the will to advance can be employed productively by family of origin members, to help each understand what it means to be an adopted person, a birth mother or a birth father. Those who choose to be proactive often report that they feel better about themselves.

Identity confusion

As pointed out by Brodzinsky *et al*, "The search for self is universal and ongoing ... Our sense of who we are is influenced by every experience we have; it's changed each time our life circumstances change" (1993, p13). It is not only the major events such as birth, death and marriage, and for those so affected, adoption, but also the summation of lesser happenings, such as each compliment or rejection, achievement or failure that add to how we feel about ourselves. Brodzinsky *et al* continue: "... adoptees have a particularly complex task in their search for self. When you live with your biological family, you have guideposts to help you along. You can see bits of your own future reflected in your parents, pieces of your own personality echoed in your brothers and sisters. There are fewer such clues for someone who is adopted" (*ibid*). 'Genealogical bewilderment' is a term that is sometimes used to describe this dilemma. Jayne Schooler (1995, p166) reports on work by Brodzinsky, in which he points out that we have different identities in different contexts, *eg* an occupational identity, a religious identity, an identity as the member of a family, etc. An individual integrates these various aspects of the self, including elements related to family. For an adult adopted person, there is a complication, for they have three families – one that they know, and two, the families of the respective birth parents, that they do not know. One adopted person expresses this marrow-deep hunger for identity, related to heritage, accompanied, in this case, by a desire to be accepted, as "I yearn for a time [when] adoptees won't be judged for wanting to be whole" (ARCS, 2004, p4).

Lifton notes that in order to survive family complexities, adopted persons assume dual identities.

> "Early on they get the message that they cannot grieve for their lost kin but must commit themselves to the identity of the adoptive clan if they are to keep the adoptive parent's love. Already abandoned by the birth mother, the child feels no choice but to abandon her, and by so doing, abandon his real self. This early potential self that is still attached to the birth mother is unacceptable to the adoptive parents and, therefore, must become unacceptable to the child ... The child forced to give up the real self cannot develop feelings of belonging ... Adopted children often try to shut out the subject of adoption. This means that they must separate one part of the self from the rest of the self" (2002, p210).

Within the adopted child, Lifton identifies

> "... the Artificial Self and the Forbidden Self, neither of which is completely true or completely false. The Artificial Self seems like the perfect child because she is so eager to please. She is compliant, puts everyone's needs before her own, and suppresses her anger. But deep inside she feels like a fake and

an imposter, feelings that may overwhelm her as an adult. Having cut off a vital part of herself, she sometimes feels dead. The Forbidden Self is more difficult. Refusing to please, he becomes oppositional, often acting out antisocially as a way of feeling alive. An adoptee may switch from one self to the other during various stages of the life cycle. The perfect child may express her or his anger in adulthood. And the Forbidden Self may eventually become a dutiful son or daughter" (*ibid*).

Verrier terms these coping strategies the False Self – defence mechanisms employed by the child to deal with the loss of the part of their Self that was wounded before he or she began "to separate [their] own identity from that of [the] mother, ... leaving the infant with a feeling of incompleteness or lack of wholeness" (1993, p38).

For adopted persons, there is another layer that adds to the complexity. The issuing of a second birth certificate, which replaces the names they were given at birth with new names, teaches adopted persons that their identity can be discarded. As Robinson points out, "Giving them a 'new' (*ie* false) identity suggests to them that who they actually are is unacceptable and must be hidden" (2004, p189).

Within adopted families, not belonging may be obvious.

"Often an undeniable fact that an adoptee does not resemble family members stimulates intense feelings of aloneness. Steve Harris, for example, did not look anything like his family. 'I would go to family reunions and everyone was tall and thin and I was short and stocky. They had dark complexions and I was much lighter ... I would spend a week with people who were supposed to be family, but we didn't have anything in common. I looked different. My personality and temperament were different. I would come home feeling like I didn't belong' " (Hochman *et al*, 1998, p12).

Samantha, in *issues*, Number 13, of Jan–Mar 1999 speaks of a similar experience. "I used to ... get up in the morning and look at my face [in the mirror], then go and have breakfast with people that seemed to be total strangers. I guess that ... I never felt as though I really belonged. Not just because of my looks, but everything about me" (p16). Samantha then reveals the antithesis: "At the age of 20, I found my uncle; the minute he opened the door he knew who I was." Later she meets her birth mother. "I could see physical resemblances ... the same coloured skin and hair, and the extroverted personalities ... I had found a very big part of myself to identify with" (*ibid*).

For birth parents also there is the potential for identity confusion. They are the two people who conceived the child, so they are the mother and the father. However, the adoptive parents who raise the child are also a mother and a father. Because they do not raise the child, some birth parents have difficulty acknowledging biological and genetic facts. In some circumstances, the confusion may have had its roots in the claim made at the time of the adoption that the adoptive parents were henceforth the 'real' parents. However, the original roles and the fundamental connections with birth parents do not disappear when the child is placed with another family. There are no such persons as a former mother and a former father.

For birth mothers, there is what is called the 'double bind', which affects their identity as a mother: " 'If you love your child you will give [him] up.' Then when they do, they are told, 'You've given [him] up, so you don't love [him] and you've no right to know anything more about [him]' " (Griffith, 1991, Section 5, p9).

Some of the birth mothers in Jones' study report trying to change their exterior, to become the 'perfect woman' to rectify their indiscretion. One, Sue, says "I was determined to make up for everything I'd done wrong. I was obsessed with trying to be a 'good girl' again, to regain my self-image" (1993, p91). Jones notes further that for many of birth mothers, as an essential part of their identity, their "self-esteem had been destroyed" by the relinquishment (p110).

Birth fathers' issues with their identity may centre on their right to call themselves a father because they did not fulfil the roles of providing for and watching over their child. They may feel that because they were not at the birth or outside the hospital, their claim to be the father is diminished.

Search and Recovery

To progress beyond loss and grief requires a mindset shift for each member of the family of origin – from reacting to the parent–child separation to taking action to address the consequences of adoption. If no effort is made to address the fundamental issues, the individual risks remaining static, possibly consumed (whether recognised or not) by the responses to grief. In my opinion, this is an unacceptable risk, one, that if chosen, prevents recovery and personal growth.

Robinson applies dual meanings to 'recovery'. The first refers to healing the emotional pain caused by adoption separation, as it applies to an individual. The second aspect addresses the situation where separated members of the family of origin are reunited; they are 'recovering' the relationship that was interrupted by the adoption (2004, Introduction). Both components are displayed in Figure 1.

The self

Mending the hurt self takes courage. It requires, firstly an acknowledgment that the original separation of birth parent and adopted child has caused damage. Then, there needs to be a commitment on the part of the individual to focus on the wounds, objectively and with the intention of learning from their effects, rather than blaming others for their original infliction. Those who choose to remain bitter about their adoption experience, by, for example being intent on compensation for advice given or actions taken on their behalf decades earlier, stifle their own recovery. The key to healing is to accept responsibility for personal actions, past and present; devolving this to others cannot promote personal development. These, the necessary ingredients of the 'search' phase, are the foundations for 'recovery'. For adopted persons and birth parents alike, personal healing represents, as Robinson puts it, "freeing up the energy that has been tied up in suppressing their grief ... If personal recovery work is not undertaken, then those affected by adoption separation can remain locked into denial and the anxiety which results from it" (2004, p21). The advice offered in Butler-Bowdon may assist: "The best way of overcoming fear is to be curious about that which you fear" (2001, p266).

Robinson places personal recovery on two levels. "On an intellectual level, you are aiming to understand what happened and on an emotional level, you are aiming to get in touch with how you feel about what happened" (2004, p22). For birth parents, recovery work may profitably include consideration of their family upbringing, the values that were the foundation of the family (including how much children were appreciated for their own sake), the relationship they had with their parents, how the family dealt with internal and external changes that occurred, the prevailing social attitudes, how news of the out-of-wedlock pregnancy was disclosed and received, who made the decisions that led to the adoption and whose interests was the separation of parent and child deemed to serve. It is also beneficial to explore the impact that the initial loss caused by the adoption has had on personal life afterwards, as well as the repercussions for relationships within the family and with others, the effects on self-esteem and the ability to trust other people, the consequences for decision-making and the capacity to deal with subsequent losses. An appreciation of the evolution of community attitudes towards out-of-wedlock conceptions may also be helpful. Telling your story, whether orally or in writing may assist with the release of feelings previously suppressed by disenfranchised grief. Support groups, attended by people with similar experiences, may help validate your personal narrative. Some people may choose to share more. Beyond the fruitful oral sharing, writing about my adoption experience has helped me not only to understand the influential events and their background, but also made me feel better about myself. At the most fundamental level, exploring the meaning of your adoption experience represents the processing of the grief and its manifestations, which occurred as a consequence of the splitting of the family of origin. Healing is possible when the impacts of the original separation and loss are comprehended and incorporated into the individual's life. This is reinforced by Phillips, who writes: "Until I could recognize my loss and allow my grief to surface, I was incapable of developing a trusting relationship or having a healthy marriage" (2004, p154).

For adopted persons, their personal healing might usefully focus on how they reacted to discovering that they were adopted and what it was like for them to grow up in their adoptive family. It may also prove productive for them if they incorporate an investigation of the evolution of social attitudes to adoption. To aid their progression, Verrier has a general word of advice for adopted persons. She advocates "sharing yourself with those close to you" (2003, p62). However, for this communication to be effective, "It means first learning who you are, so that you can share your authentic self and not that false self you fashioned out of trauma-based behavior that at one time helped you to cope" (*ibid*). As Robinson puts it, with advice for all members of the family of origin,

> "When you have a sense that you have achieved a level of acceptance of the issues surrounding your adoption separation experience, it is likely that you will feel more comfortable sharing your experience with others ... If you are able to present your experience to others in a powerful and confident manner, then you will find that you no longer feel the sense of

shame and guilt that you may have felt prior to undertaking personal recovery work" (2004, p38)

and

"Whether or not a reunion takes place ... personal recovery work plays a vital role in the journey towards healing for those who have experienced an adoption separation" (*ibid*).

Anecdotal evidence suggests that few people regret undertaking personal healing, whether or not it leads to the next stage – reunion.

Parent and child reunion

For most people, personal healing provides the catalyst to seek reunion. Those who have 'gone inside' are usually well placed to progress to meeting the person from whom they were separated by adoption. These persons may have addressed the associated feelings, resulting perhaps in diminished anger, guilt and sorrow and so understand the impact of adoption upon themselves.

It is more likely that those who initiate searches will have seized the opportunity to undertake personal recovery tasks. On this basis, the searcher may enjoy an advantage. For those who are the subject of searches, the invitation to participate in reunion presents an opportunity for interpersonal recovery, which may provide a catalyst to initiate or to re-invigorate personal recovery work. Sometimes, as in the case of Evelyn Robinson and her son Stephen, individual searches, without the knowledge of the other, are concurrent (Robinson, 2003). In their case, each performed independent personal recovery work, paving the way for mutually sought interpersonal healing.

Reunion represents a part of the quest for wholeness, or, as Lifton puts it, in the case of adopted persons, the "need for biological, historical, and human connectedness" (1994, p128).

Persons separated by adoption can make significant contributions to their own well-being and that of the other party by agreeing to participate in reunion. Again, this is reinforced by Lifton, who asserts that "empowerment and reconnection are the core experiences of recovery" (1994, p128).

The healing can be viewed at two levels. Firstly, both parent and child are part of each other's identity. Every child embodies the genetic characteristics passed on by their mother and their father, whether or not they become an adopted person. The mother and the father (in the case of an adoption, the birth father and the birth mother) pass on their genes to the child. It is natural for any child separated from their parents to wish to know their heritage. As a corollary, I believe it is natural, as with any parent, for birth mothers and birth fathers to wish to meet and spend time with the person to whom they are intimately related and to whom they have bequeathed their genes. Typically, birth parents are precluded from participating in the joys of the day-to-day parenting of their adopted child. This heightened sense of having 'missed out' reinforces the birth parents' imperative to find the part of their legacy and their lives that is 'missing'. The second component is the grief caused by the original separation; reunion represents an opportunity to integrate the loss and its consequences into three lives and thus provide mending for all.

The focal point of recovery may differ for each participant. The baby who subsequently becomes an adopted person was carried by the birth mother for nine months before the birth. During this period, a bond with psychological, genetic and biological elements was established. The birth father is linked to his offspring genetically and, assuming he is aware of the presence of the child, psychologically. When an adopted child is separated from his mother and father, he is removed (at best temporarily) from his genetic markers, such as facial features, body language, talents and basic personality, facets of the gene pool provided by the birth parents. An infant, because of the bond forged during pregnancy does know his mother and instinctively wants to be with her. It is to be expected that for adopted persons, issues surrounding their identity, including perhaps the perception that they were not good enough for their birth mother to keep, are the focus of their recovery. This fundamental search for identity may in part explain why it is more common for adopted persons to initiate searches for their birth parents, usually the birth mother, than vice versa.

MacKay, placing her focus on the benefits of recovery, opines that "the act of searching and/or maintaining a relationship with the birth family reclaims the adoptee's autonomy, power and equality" (2005, p18). Lifton acknowledges that for adopted persons, whatever the degree of healing, "after search and reunion, at least they have a potential for growth" (1994, p272). I maintain that the same maxim applies to birth parents.

For the birth mother who has lost her baby, it is likely that the grief that results from being separated from her child will be the focal point of her pain and her healing. Her feeling of loss is immediate, acute and likely to increase over time. A birth father's responses may be more complex. His relationship with the birth mother was actual, at the very least physical and, based on published studies, often affectional. He may never have seen his child, if his relationship with the birth mother ended before the birth, or if he was absent in the period between the birth and the adoption. His child may not have the tangible presence experienced by the birth mother. It may be years later that the separation from his child is acknowledged emotionally by the birth father, as he realises that what he has lost is the opportunity to participate daily in the life of the child he has never seen. His sense of loss may lie dormant, but when realised, become profound. Towards the birth mother he knew, a birth father's reaction is more likely be centred on guilt, a perception that he has let her down, causing the mother–child bond to be broken and this may become the core of the reconciliation and the mending he seeks with the birth mother. The birth mother's reciprocal reaction, if she feels that she was forsaken, may be anger towards the birth father.

Schooler (1995) issues a cautionary note about the expression of anger during reunion. "[The birth mother] may be angry with her family or her boyfriend (at the time) for not helping her when she needed it most. She may be angry with herself for not being stronger and standing up for what she truly wanted – to keep her child ... all that anger could manifest itself in anger toward the adoptee ... when she's really angry about what she's remembering" (p145) and "this anger is never for the person. It is an anger for a situation that was out of their control" (p143). She also refers to the release of guilt and shame: "The pressures of family, clergy, social workers and society created the belief that women who were pregnant out of marriage and surrendered their child were worthless ... Many ... are not able to get past ... the accompanying shame when found by their ... child. When contact is made by the ... child, old feelings of shame and guilt rush to the surface" (pp142–143).

In her study, Jones (1993) observes that "Many birthmothers emphasized that reunion was *not* a cure for the regrets, angers, or grief they faced after relinquishing. Reunion had, in fact, offered additional risks of rejection, disappointment, and confrontation with the events, issues, and emotions of the past" (p211) [emphasis in the reference]. It took courage to face these matters. Other birth mothers "were compelled to resume the grieving they'd abandoned years ago and to confront the toll relinquishing had taken on their lives" (Jones, 1993, p206). It is possible that a number of these women had not undertaken personal recovery work as preparation for the possibility of reunion. Overall, says Jones, "With reunions, risks were taken, secrets were revealed, truths were confronted" as a result of which, "Although reunions often emphasized the losses of the past, they also offered opportunities for the birthmothers and their [separated] children to salvage their futures" (1993, p229). Jones concludes that healing was possible because many birth mothers allowed "themselves to grieve and mourn, to seek support and help when they need[ed] it [and] to assert themselves as individuals" (1993, p287).

Robinson (2004) contends that "many of those who have experienced an adoption separation are seeking a form of grief resolution" (p43). She also "[believes] that it is appropriate for reunion between family members separated by adoption to be encouraged and promoted" (p41) and concludes that "Reunion represents the loss of ignorance and fear. Reunion can replace ignorance with knowledge and fear with confidence" (p42). Robinson then sounds a warning for those who enter reunion without preparatory work: "If ... no attempt at personal recovery has been made before the reunion event takes place, then the impact often seems to be greater, as the grief has been dormant for a longer period of time and has not already been processed, even in part. I believe that this is why many reunion experiences resemble bereavement situations and can cause major grieving behaviours to be exhibited" (2004, p50). These emotions include sadness, numbness, anger, guilt and fear (Robinson, 2004, p51), all identified as outcomes of the original separation.

Usually, it is impossible to know beforehand what stage the sought person has reached in their healing. It is likely that the person who initiates the reunion believes that they are ready to meet the person from whom they were separated. However, they may encounter a person who denies that separation has affected their life, or one who realises that they have many yet unresolved issues to address for themselves. Even in the circumstance where the initiator is, believing they have it 'all together', reunited with a person who has an awareness of their own separation issues, it is certain that the reunion will raise emotional issues that an individual working alone cannot resolve.

Robinson (2004, p61) identifies four possible reunion outcomes. There are those who successfully complete the mourning tasks and incorporate the adoption experience into their lives. There are those who enter the reunion, but choose not to perform the mourning tasks and so retain the loss and associated grief as unresolved issues. There are those who want to reach out for reunion but cannot proceed because the other person is unavailable to them, through death, a failure to be located or a refusal to participate. Finally, there is the situation where neither party is willing to enter reunion, confront their grief and accept the benefits that working together can bring. Of the four, only the first is a productive result for both parties. It signifies that both participants have recognised the benefits of openness and the potential for recovery. As anybody separated by an adoption knows, there is a likelihood of outreach, but it is the preparedness of each individual to accept the possibility of reunion and see it as an opportunity for healing and personal growth that governs their choices and determines the outcome. In the second situation above, when the parties meet, progress is compromised because the fundamental issues resulting from the initial separation are not addressed. The third and fourth scenarios involve persons who are not (yet) ready to acknowledge the missing part of themselves and the importance of the other. For those who choose not to participate in reunion, there can be long term negative consequences. The grief, whether or not acknowledged, remains a burden and a barrier to personal growth. According to Robinson (2004, p65), a person in denial may suffer physical symptoms or engage in aberrant behaviour. To suppress the pain, some may turn to drugs or alcohol, whilst others avoid contact by relocating physically to a distant place.

The matter of trust, displayed as wariness or even jealousy, may become an issue for spouses when contact and reunion occur. Anecdotal evidence suggests that the husband or wife of an adopted person, the wife of a birth father and the husband of a birth mother may experience difficulties accepting the inclusion of the returning family of origin member into the fold. Members of families separated by an adoption have a bond based on consanguinity; the spouse is related to the initiator or recipient of contact by marriage only. It is no surprise that the spouse might feel left out as parent and child (or in the case of birth parents re-establishing contact, mother and father) enter reunion. Carlene Wood (personal communication, 2004) offers the observation that reactions are sometimes more intense if the entrant into the family is of the same gender as the spouse, *eg* a wife may feel threatened by contact initiated by her birth father husband's daughter. However, if a spouse allows space and displays generosity towards their partner, as they address the loss and the grief issues that resulted from the original separation, this is sure to be appreciated.

By definition, a reunion is between members of the family of origin. Other people, related either directly by marriage or through adoption, did not experience the original separation, so cannot be reunited. Friends and interested others are also observers, not participants. All these people, in particular the spouse, and in the case of adopted persons, the adoptive parents, do, however, have a critical role to play – providing unconditional support for those contemplating or engaged in reunion. Anderson has this to say about the contribution of adoptive parents: "When [they] ... give support and understanding, they give their children freedom, and with it the knowledge that they love and respect both their children and themselves" (1997, p9). I contend that the thrust of this statement applies also to what loving spouses can offer.

Whilst a great deal of satisfaction and inner peace can be achieved through personal healing, reunion represents an investment in restoring a lost relationship. It is a relationship that is centred on loss, but realises the benefits of 'finding' not only one's self but also the other person. It is important, however, to remind ourselves about the role of personal responsibility. We cannot ask the person from whom we were separated by adoption to be responsible for mending us, for this can be construed by them as blame for our predicament. At best, such a request is tantamount to asking the other person to own our personal issues. We are each responsible for our own healing, whether or not reunion takes place. If the reunion does not meet expectations, then we can choose to take what was offered and apply it to our personal recovery.

Ultimately, it is only through taking personal responsibility that those separated by adoption can achieve reunion, as well as resolve identity issues.

Identity settlement

Because taking ownership of one's actions, whether or not it results in reunion, has an impact on how an individual perceives himself or herself, both personal and interpersonal recovery can have an impact on 'identity'.

Schooler (1995) records the reactions of adopted persons: "Because of our reunion, my life is richer and fuller" (p190) and "Searching felt like the biggest risk I've ever taken in my life, yet I couldn't be complete without knowing" (p191). Robinson (2004) includes a personal message from her son, in which he writes, that as a result of reunion, "I personally feel much more whole. I now have a fuller understanding of my origins and therefore of who I am." Mary Keller states "Connecting with my birth family has given me a sense of completion ... and the knowledge of my own story" (Blau, 1993, p100). These individual comments by adopted persons reinforce the conclusions reached by others. Brodzinsky *et al* note that "the consolidation of identity" is an important outcome of searching (1993, p145). Marshall and McDonald (2001, p245) record that, from an Australian study of the reunion experiences of adopted persons, identity issues, related to "the knowledge they had gained about themselves and their family background" emerged as a critical factor. Stephanie Mello, in Blau (1993) summarises the benefits of identity settlement for adopted persons – "to help [them] understand themselves better, to feel stronger and more confident" (p29). From the other side of a reunion, birth mother Debra Warila records, that when she met her son, "I had this feeling of completeness or wholeness, and that feeling has stayed" (Blau, 1993, p82). At the most fundamental level, a birth parent may recognise that reunion provides an opportunity for them to confirm their status as the progenitors of their child, an element of their identity that they perhaps had questioned in the aftermath of the adoption.

In his account of the experiences of birth fathers, Gary Clapton notes that, for those men who had been or were in contact with their child, the majority "experienced improved self-esteem" (2003, p174). One birth mother in Jones concludes that "I have more self-esteem because I searched ... I feel better about myself because I finally stopped holding in my grief and took action ... I *did* something to relieve my misery and declare my presence in the world" (1993, p199) [emphasis in the original].

For some people, mending deliberately involves all members of the family of origin *ie* the birth mother and the child, as well as the birth father. In their study of reunion, Gediman and Brown record "that several women achieved more complete senses of resolution when their sons and daughters met their birthfathers: feelings that unfinished business had been taken care of and that the circle, finally, was closed" (1991, p182). Sometimes members of the families of the respective birth parents, *eg* half-siblings, play a role. Birth mother Patricia Taylor records the benefits of working with the children of her marriage, the half-siblings of Kathi. "The recovery process has involved us all as we move to replenish self esteem (*sic*)" (1995, p294).

Increased self-esteem may in turn provide a useful lens through which to view the past in a more realistic light. An acknowledgment of loss and the processing of grief may allow the recovered person to view their past actions and reactions from a different, more honest perspective. For example, a birth mother may now accept that at the time of the adoption she was not stupid or negligent, but rather, naive. Instead of feeling inherently bad for allowing the adoption to take place, both birth parents may acknowledge that at the time, they were powerless; the life-changing decision was made for, not by them. This clarity may further enhance how they, today, feel about themselves, without in any way diminishing their recognition of the consequences of an adoption for all parties.

Speaking from the perspective of a birth mother, Sandra Falconer Pace (2004b) both laments the paucity of community awareness and summarises the path to recovery and its relationship to shame, grief and identity, when she writes:

> "As more of us who lost our children talk about our lifelong pain, it will be easier for all of us to set aside the bonds of shame. It will become easier to let go the trauma and anguish. It will take longer for our circle to set aside grief unresolved through all the years our children are lost to us, longer than those who don't experience it can understand. Our feelings have been disrespected and underestimated for decades. It may be that the enormity of the loss can never be resolved, only embraced as part of our identity. As we find our way to healing, as we let go of the pain and reclaim lives unshadowed by shame, we can welcome our children with joy and lighter hearts."

Adoptive and birth parents

It is a fact that an adopted person has two sets of parents. Post-reunion, it may be helpful for an adult adopted person to consider facilitating communication between his or her adoptive and birth parents. From the stance of an adoptive parent, Verrier observes "Many of the traits that you may have admired in your child can probably be found in some members of the birth family ... Get[ting] to know as many members of the birth family as possible ... will help you know and understand the ... personality of your child" (2003, p277).

Through meeting the adoptive parents, the individual birth parents may be able to fill in some of the information gaps for the period when the child was missing from their lives. Jim Shinn, a birth father, reports that he has "a really good relationship with [his son's] adoptive family," because "they are very open" (Blau, 1993, p125).

The view from support groups

In Melbourne, the Australian city in which I live, I have attended many support group meetings. I return, because, in this forum, I continue to learn about the legacy of adoption. After a decade, I have reached some general conclusions that apply to the two main groups of participants. For birth mothers, overwhelmingly adoption represents loss, especially of their child. Other emotional responses radiate from this, their primary wound. Adopted persons often appear to be lost – to be disoriented and searching for their Self, a manifestation of the primal wound (the term used by Verrier, 1993 to describe the trauma suffered by the infant, as the result of being separated from his or her mother, soon after birth). I have noticed that many adopted persons have difficulty telling their story as a cohesive experience. Instead, they present a kaleidoscope of loose threads, which, it becomes apparent eventually, are interconnected. I have detected that whilst birth mothers often begin their (linear) narrative with the birth and departure of their child, adopted persons often labour to select a starting point, which perhaps is not surprising, given that they have no cognitive awareness of being separated from their birth parents. Bewilderment is less obvious amongst those adopted persons who have performed some recovery work, centred on their heritage and their identity. For birth mothers and adopted persons alike, these observations from support groups confirm a direct correlation between, in the first instance, separation and wounding, and then later, as a result of dedicated effort, integration and healing.

The third essay in this section focusses on the consequences of separation for the birth parents. As far as I am aware, previously this perspective has not been presented in any detail. I point out the benefits of closure for the birth mother and the birth father.

3. Love's labour's lost

In discussions about the impact of adoption, there is another separation and reunion pairing that is frequently forgotten, or in some instances, deliberately ignored. It involves the two parents – the birth mother and the birth father. This oversight is not congruent with the events that resulted in an adoption. An adult male and an adult female each contributed to the conception of the child. The mother carried the child through pregnancy, as a result of which she typically forged physical and emotional bonds with her unborn infant. An outcome of the in-utero bonding is that often the primary reunion sought is between the mother and her now adult child. Frequently, the reunion between father and child is secondary, *ie* it occurs after the reunion between mother and child. Given the fewer links a father has with his child, this common hierarchy is to be expected.

Whilst I acknowledge that the quality of the original relationship between birth parents covers a broad spectrum, ranging from coercion to love, my accent here is on those relationships in which genuine, reciprocated affection was a feature. I accept, from listening to and reading the accounts of birth mothers that affectional relationships are not necessarily the norm. However, anecdotal evidence suggests that there are a considerable number of birth parents who not only have positive, lingering thoughts for the other, but also consider the possibility of seeking closure.

Transparent

The birth mother and the birth father often separate (unless they later marry each other) at or about the time of the adoption. The reasons for this split are various. The mother may not have wanted the birth father to be involved. The birth father may have withdrawn his support. Social workers may have intervened and deliberately excluded the birth father from discussions about parenting. The two sets of parents may have made the decisions about the future of their children and their grandchild. As a consequence, the birth parents may feel that they relinquished control of their relationship to others; that this was against their wills and perhaps pushed them apart.

Some birth mothers and birth fathers may be envious of other couples who, faced with similar circumstances, kept their children. In these cases, the intervention of parents who sanctioned marriage (or in some cases insisted that the father and mother of the child get married) after the pregnancy became known, but before the child was born, resulted in a first child whose date of birth was less than nine months after the wedding. Whilst this situation often carried a stigma, particularly before the final quarter of the twentieth century, any disgrace tended to evaporate with time. Although the circumstances of the child's conception and birth may have created ructions within the extended families of both parents, nevertheless an adoption was avoided. Birth parents may be disappointed that they too did not have supportive families.

Affectional bonds exist within many relationships. When they are broken, they sometimes leave a residue of regret and missed opportunities. However, in situations where the couple create a child, and that child is lost to adoption, the presence of the third person, as evidence of intimacy between two adults, can be a potent reminder of the relationship that once existed between the birth mother and the birth father. Lovers who separate without having conceived a child lack the same reminder of the former affectional bond. Lovers who conceive a child and stay together see and appreciate the evidence of their intimacy every day.

Where a significant relationship has been interrupted by an adoption, it is to be anticipated that the birth parents will have 'unfinished business'. Not only are there bonds between each of the parents and their child, but an affectional bond may persist between the birth mother and the birth father. These tripartite connections represent the Triple Bond (Coles, 2004). Because an adoption sometimes coincides with the breaking of a meaningful adult relationship, it is reasonable to expect that the separated birth parents too will experience post-adoption suffering.

Parting

The two adults of a severed relationship, the birth mother and the birth father, suffer losses. There is the loss of each to the other, as a physical parting. For some birth parents, the relationship may have been fleeting or perhaps the child was conceived as the result of rape. For others, there may be the loss of a serious relationship, often, according to studies by researchers such as Harkness (1991), Nicholls and Levy (1992), Carlini (1993), Clapton (2003) and Witney (2003), one that has spanned years. Depending on the circumstances that led to the pregnancy and the degree of involvement by the father in the decisions that led to the adoption, there may be a loss of trust, or at the very least, profound disappointment, experienced by the birth mother.

Both birth parents may grieve their separation, particularly if their parting was in a situation that did not allow closure. It is documented in the literature that often the adoption is arranged by the parents of one or both of the birth parents. The birth mother and birth father may not only be excluded from the decision-making but also 'banned' from seeing each other again. The grief that they experience may be disenfranchised. Residual feelings between birth parents are unlikely to be sanctioned by the community. Nor is the public likely to condone the open mourning of the loss of a relationship that might otherwise have culminated in marriage. In such circumstances the birth parents' grief may feel like a 'hole' in their lives. Jones is one author who acknowledges this form of "unresolved grief" (1993, p133).

Guilt may be an issue for both birth parents. A birth mother may feel that, in the face of parental disapproval, she failed to champion the man who wanted to marry her. She may consider that her lack of resolve not only damaged a loving relationship, but also, as a result, made it difficult for her to contemplate keeping her child. If the birth mother decides to act alone, she may feel guilty for excluding the birth father, of not providing him with the opportunity to participate in decisions about his child's future. A birth father who was unable to stand by the birth mother, either of his own volition or because of external pressures, may experience guilt for having let down the birth mother. In each case, it is the parent who feels they were unable to include the other who bears the brunt of the burden of guilt.

Whilst for a birth mother, father and child are discrete persons about whom often she can make separate decisions on the future of the respective relationships, a birth father's single decision necessarily embraces mother and child, for, by virtue of her pregnancy, the mother is carrying the child. A birth father may experience 'double jeopardy', in the sense that he suffers twice for the one action (Coles, 2004, p109). He may feel that either his weakness or determination not to stand by the mother has consigned two people to their fates. It is likely, because of the in-utero bond that a birth mother establishes with her child prior to the birth, that the focus of her loss and associated feelings will be on the child.

A birth father's reaction to loss is perhaps more likely to focus on mother and child as one. Because his relationship was with the woman and there is no father–child physical connection, during the pregnancy the man may find it difficult to look beyond the mother who is carrying the child. After the adoption, the birth father may realise that the child has a presence and that he has been responsible for breaking the bond between mother and child. This comprehension can perhaps further reinforce his guilt, particularly if the father has had the opportunity to see his infant after the birth and before the adoption. For the majority of birth fathers who do not see their new-born baby, their conscious connection with the actual events may remain centred on the person whom they knew and let down – the mother. This phenomenon perhaps explains why some birth fathers begin their interpersonal recovery work by seeking reconciliation with the mother of their child. (In my case, I felt that to make progress at a personal level, I first needed to seek rapprochement with Kay.)

Jones notes that, even in circumstances where the birth parents married after the adoption, "many found that their marriages were haunted by the past ... the loss of their first child tended to make their happiness incomplete" (1993, p131). Jones continues, observing that "marriages between birthmothers and birthfathers were often speckled (*sic*) with scars and unhealed wounds from relinquishment" (p133).

A birth mother may be angry with the birth father because he has not stood by her. In other cases, the target of her anger could be her parents if they intervened and forbad the involvement of the birth father in decisions about the future of their child. Perhaps her anger is self-directed, if she believes that she failed to protect the birth father from the slings and arrows projected by her family and others. A birth father may feel anger towards the parents, both his and the birth mother's, if they prevented him from supporting or having access to the birth mother. His anger might surface against himself for not assisting the birth mother. Some birth fathers express anger towards the birth mother, because they believe that she did not do enough to prevent their child from being adopted. Both birth parents may direct their anger against the constraints and the stigmatisation that society imposed upon them.

The impact of the loss of a child to adoption on subsequent intimacy is well documented in the literature. What has been overlooked is the effect the loss of a meaningful adult relationship upon intimacy. If the plans for the birth mother and the birth father to marry were thwarted or reversed, it is no surprise that the outcomes might be a loss of faith in commitment and perhaps sincerity. In this situation, it is not only the loss of a child but a wariness about entering subsequent deep, long relationships that may occupy the minds of one or both birth parents and condition their approach to intimacy with others. Put another way, it may be the severing of the original adult relationship, not the adoption, which, for each birth parent has the greater influence on subsequent intimacy. If the original relationship between the birth parents was coercive, then the birth mother may be wary of intimacy with men. Here the quality of one uncaring relationship may again condition her attitude to future intimate relationships.

According to Jones, "Some [birthmothers] felt so deeply tied to the birthfathers that, even if they were no longer in contact, they could not allow any other men, even their own husbands, to come close" (1993, p110). By contrast, Clapton notes that in the circumstance where birth parents subsequently married each other, "All of the men talked of relationship difficulties arising from either an inability to discuss the adoption experience or their personal distress" (2003, p140). In this case, the loss of their child creates communication issues within the marriage.

The fear of a rebuff, resulting from the circumstances of the original separation or a consideration of present relationships (*eg* does the spouse of their former sexual partner know about the child?), may inhibit one birth parent approaching the other to resolve outstanding issues surrounding their separation and the adoption.

Control may be employed by each birth parent to compensate for the disempowerment they experienced when the adoption took place and they, as a man and a woman savouring a significant relationship, were separated. This may manifest itself in a need to be in control of subsequent relationships, to avoid the risk of being hurt by the actions of another influential person, in this case, their partner.

Most fundamentally, the parting of the birth parents can have a profound impact on their perceptions of themselves as mothers, fathers, lovers and worthy persons, core elements of their identity as individual human beings.

A lingering residual affection between the birth parents may heighten the common responses to separation and loss. The spectre of 'what might have been' can, unless managed by each birth parent, become both a magnet and an obstacle, which the birth father and the birth mother may find to be insurmountable.

Clapton concludes, from his study of thirty birth fathers in the United Kingdom, that "For a considerable proportion of the men, ... the birth mother lived on in their feelings ..." (2003, p139). Stromberg found that when she interviewed a group of North American birth fathers, their "positive attitudes towards birth mothers" was a persistent theme (2002, p61), represented by "intense feelings and a remarkable amount of compassion" (p64). Writing from the other side of the severed relationship, Jones records that "a number of birthmothers hoped someday to resurrect and restore the loving relationship with the birthfathers that had perished under the traumas of relinquishment" (1993, pp234–235). However, notes Jones, not all dissolved relationships fall into this category; for some birth mothers the birth fathers "represented threatening, unsettling unfinished business" (p233).

Frequently, the motives for reconnecting are related to the conception and the shared contribution the birth parents have made to their child's heritage. One of the birth mothers in Gediman and Brown concludes that "her revived interest in the birthfather was connected to the bond they shared by virtue of having created this child" (1991, p180).

Reconciliation

Seldom are the results of the reunion between birth parents recorded. I have described my reunion with Kay, the birth mother of our son (Coles, 2004). A little has been written from the perspective of the birth mother.

Jones (1993) observes that many birth mothers found birth fathers who had experienced a "familiar array of guilty feelings and anxieties" (p242), including "incomplete grief, avoidance of intimacy, difficulties in parenting, generalized guilt and low self-esteem" (p241), feelings that resembled their own. She also refers to patterns of "loveless marriages, compulsions to be 'perfect', and children born in quick succession" (p242). Continuing, Jones records the experience of a particular birth father, from the perspective of the birth mother. "He replaced our relinquished child right away by marrying the very next girl he met and starting a family immediately. His marriage was not based on love. Like me, he married to have another child ... He *says* it's all in the past, but he still calls me a few times each year. He can't ... let go of me or our son" (p242) [emphasis in the original].

This theme of concern for mother and child is echoed by one of the birth fathers in Gediman and Brown: "He's searching for his former girlfriend and his child now because he feels he abandoned them both. He wants to make amends" (1991, p167). Cicchini (1993) and Clapton (2003) have noted similar responses amongst birth fathers and Coles (2004) has explored the ramifications of letting down the other two members of the family of origin.

In the sparse literature about the views of birth mothers on reunions with birth fathers, there is a frequently expressed reaction; one of heightened emotions surfacing, *viz*: "Several of the birthmothers we interviewed felt that dealing with the birthfather and/or their feelings about him, was the most difficult part of the post-reunion experience" (Gediman and Brown, 1991, p181) and "[for] those who remained emotionally involved with the birthfathers, [the] renewed contact with their former lovers was as wrenching as the reunions [with their child]" (Jones, 1993, p234). Specifically, "[often] the passions and intense emotions aroused by the renewed contact were downright frightening to birthparents who had survived for decades by remaining rigidly 'in control' of their lives and relationships. The prospects of taking emotional risks, making dramatic changes, or sacrificing 'normalcy' were, for many, far too threatening" (Jones, 1993, p236). Sometimes, the reactions are tinged with disappointment, *viz* "the emotional aftermath of relinquishment combined with the events of the intervening years had changed both birthparents so profoundly that, even when the desires were mutual, the chances that their relationship would succeed were minimal" (Jones, 1993, p235).

For those who have performed no or little personal recovery work, reunion represents the first opportunity for suppressed grief to surface, bringing with it a plethora of feelings. Even if individual birth parents have addressed how they feel about themselves and their role in the original separation and perhaps also achieved reunion with the child, there are likely to be additional matters, complicated in some cases by a suppressed love for their former sexual partner, which may erupt when the birth parents reunite.

Individual reunions have unique qualities and there is no reason to suppose that a reunion between birth parents, typically adults at the time of separation and now, should be identical to that experienced between a birth parent and their child. The fundamentals of the parent–child relationship change between the adoption and reunion, usually over a hiatus that spans at least two decades. The child who was an infant when adopted, approaches reunion as an adult. There are some reports of reunions between mother and child, both adults, in which the parties feel drawn to revert to the time when parent and baby were separated. This parent–child regression is not a factor in reunions between birth parents, for typically they parted as adults and they return as (hopefully more mature) adults. What parent–child and parent–parent reunions do have in common is that the participants have the same fundamental issues, centred on loss and grief, to address.

Some mothers have reported that reunion assists with the resolution of the relationship between the birth parents. Jones records that "Although the loss of their fantasies devastated some women, others found that the truth finally set them free" (1993, p236). Gediman and Brown note another advantage: "[birthmothers] needed to meet and talk with the birthfather to 'unclog' [their] own repressed memories" (1991, p181). I can envisage that the dialogue might profitably cover matters such as the personal, family and social circumstances at the time of conception and the adoption, as well as how each has addressed the subsequent emotional pain. Conversing provides an opportunity to ask and to answer questions.

Patricia Taylor is a birth mother who, with the birth father, Michael, welcomes the opportunity to talk "alone ... for the first time ever about our child." She assesses the benefits: "... we answered questions for each other which were still unresolved regarding the death of our relationship and the loss of our child [twenty] years before. Michael shared with me, as I did with him, the rituals he had developed over the years to deal with the loss of his daughter" (1995, p287).

As a birth father, I contend that it is never too late for birth parents to engage in a dialogue. I do acknowledge that this might not be appropriate in some circumstances, for example if the child was conceived as the result of rape, where the relationship between the birth parents is underpinned by the spectre of threatening behaviour, or if one party does not wish to participate. However, I believe this dialogue does serve a useful purpose in circumstances where both birth parents accept that it is important they resolve personal issues surrounding the loss of their child, and further, agree that the communication is integral to individual emotional healing.

Robinson proposes that if birth parents offer each other "the opportunity to address their grief issues and perform their personal recovery work ... prior to reunion with the [adult adopted person], then that adult will have the benefit of being reunited with birth parents ... who are more able to support the adopted adult child" (2004, pp79–80). In my opinion, conciliation between the birth parents reduces the possibility of an adult adopted person finding a mother and a father who bear ill-will towards each other, a distancing that may sabotage the prospects of a productive reunion between birth parent and child. Because of the potential benefits that may accrue for all three members of the family of origin, I believe it is appropriate that the first contact be between the birth mother and the birth father.

Sandra Falconer Pace (2004a), in a review of *Ever After: Fathers and the Impact of Adoption,* refers to the gains that accrued for her and her son after she made contact with the birth father. "I had carried resentment against him for the loss of our son for 27 years ... but in talking with him I realized that he also grieved for the loss of his only son. He recognized that he'd made mistakes, just as I had and also recognized ... These realizations allowed me to let go of the resentment I felt towards him. It made reunion with our son much easier, since it allowed me to speak well of him to our son." Pace's personal experience raises an important point. The birth father who appeared to be callous and uncaring during the pregnancy and/or adoption may, over time, come to regret not standing by the birth mother.

Karen (personal communication, 2005) is another who noticed a change in the birth father, when, in her case, she contacted him 35 years after the adoption. The man who had treated her harshly before her son was born now acknowledged the pain she had experienced as the result of losing her son, asked many questions about the welfare of his adult child, with whom Karen had had contact, and was pleased to hear that he was a grandfather. For Karen the outcomes of the initial conversation were positive. She felt that she could view the father of her child in a different light; he had changed and for the better. She was relieved that the contact she had hesitated to make, because of his past behaviour, had soothed her apprehensions and brought a degree of closure for her.

In circumstances where a detailed exploration of the issues is not feasible, I recommend that birth parents consider the ritual of communicating to honour their child's birthday. Both may benefit from an annual conversation, however brief this may be. Mason reports that "Even after Randy and his son's birthmother, Kim, married other people, he and Kim continued to annually commemorate their son's birthday" (1995, p14). I cannot imagine an adopted person, whether or not presently in contact with their birth parents, being unmoved by the knowledge that the birth mother and the birth father jointly have remembered and celebrated their birthday.

For those birth mothers who feel they have nothing to admire about the birth father of their child, I suggest they consider that he may now be prepared to acknowledge the consequences of his actions. This softening of attitude may allow both birth parents, and ultimately the child, to achieve positive outcomes. Forgiveness and the benefit of the doubt can provide cleared paths to healing, if exercised. For the birth father who was absent when the child was placed for adoption, the consequences of him now owning his actions and saying 'sorry' should not be underestimated. At the very least, it would be unhelpful to dismiss his atonement outright.

Furthermore, I recommend that birth fathers who left the relationship with the birth mother before or at the time of the adoption, not expecting to hear from her again, respond considerately to her outreach, made many years later. Through his receptiveness, the birth father may assist her healing. Her initiative may also allow him to recall and to come to terms with his role in the events that culminated in the adoption of their child.

There are birth parents who do not need to re-establish contact with one another, because they are married. Jones observes that "Some birthparent couples communicated openly, sharing their feelings about relinquishment, and searched for their children together. Others, however, did not. Occasionally birthmothers searched independently, compelled to separate their needs to find their children from their husbands' needs to suppress or deny the past" (1993, p238). Jones then offers a salient conclusion: "Most whose husbands protested their searches said that the birthfathers had neither grieved for their surrendered children nor supported the [birthmothers] in their own grief" (*ibid*). This demonstrable support embraces reunion, as well. On the subject of husbands, this time referring to those who do not have an adoption experience of their own, Jones writes of their key role: "Birthmothers who are happily married usually attribute their happiness, at least in part, to their husbands' unreserved acceptance of their pasts and support of their efforts to cope with their feelings" (1993, p137).

Jones has an overall conclusion about interpersonal recovery, as it applies to the seventy-two birth mothers she studied, *viz*, "By renewing contact and tending to long-festering wounds, some birthparents were able to acknowledge each other's pain and help each other to heal. When this occurred, reunions between birthparents were, in their own way, just as important as those shared with their children" (1993, p243). With reference to the reunion between birth parents and based on personal experience, I agree, wholeheartedly.

I can see the benefits of the two birth parents, as mature adults, engaging in a dialogue, thus bringing life's experiences to their discussion about loss, grief and healing. However, it is my view that there is no substitute for making decisions in the first instance that would have kept an inceptive family together and so prevented an adoption.

Thus far, this essay has addressed the separation and mending between parent and child and the two birth parents as distinct events. There is, I suggest, a final step, that of reconciling the complete family of origin. This is a process that involves mother, father and child. Inclusion can be a significant gesture for all three persons, because it has the capacity to close the interpersonal wounds caused by the adoption. This 'grand' reunion acknowledges the ties that bind the members of the birth family, the people who are joined by the Triple Bond. I am not aware of such a reunion being documented in detail, *ie* from the perspectives of the three participants. However, I do know of one example of involvement told from the viewpoint of the birth father, up to but not including a tripartite reunion. Roger Stallings is a married birth father who remains in open contact with the married birth mother of his son – "I kept up with her life and she kept up with mine" (2004, p13). He continues: "Neither of us kept any secrets from our families ... and we never once forgot his birthday" (*ibid*). When Stallings searches for and locates his adult son, "I immediately called Marianne [the birth mother] and told her ..." (2004, p14). Marianne and son Terry meet, then Stallings and Terry ("We have developed the most incredible relationship" (*ibid*)).

I know of another example of a search initiated by the birth parents acting together ("Her father and I have always been in contact"). The birth mother and the birth father have each corresponded with their daughter, but not yet achieved reunion (Steer, 2004). Taylor (1995) is one writer who acknowledges the three members of the family of origin getting together, but she does not provide details about the outcome.

I can envisage the benefits of a tripartite reconciliation, but only after the three dyads of mother and father, mother and child, and father and child have dealt with their specific separation and integration issues and now feel that they are ready to face the prospect of being, for the brief time they are together, the family that an adoption broke apart. Because this rather unusual family reunion (a triad) potentially could cause intense emotions surrounding 'what might have been' to arise, I recommend it only for participants whose personal and interpersonal healing (as dyads) is well advanced.

I maintain that significant benefits can result if the three members of the family of origin are involved in reunion. The willing participation of all provides opportunities to explore the circumstances that led to the adoption, to answer questions and to celebrate the passing of genetic characteristics from parent to child. These matters make vital contributions to identity settlement and personal healing. In my view, full reunion is not accomplished if only two of the members of the birth family are involved. The birth family comprises mother, father and child. All played some role in the events surrounding the adoption. Post-adoption, all have roles to play in the exploration and comprehension of the original separation, for all were wounded by the same episode. Individually and collectively, the birth mother, the adopted person and the birth father are the beneficiaries, if they acknowledge the Triple Bond and co-operate to heal their wounds. At a physical level, separation breaks the Triple Bond, whilst reunion presents an opportunity for these tripartite links to be repaired. More fundamentally, the birth parents and the adopted child are joined by the act of conception and by their consanguinity, as well as psychologically and emotionally. It is this inner world that presents the greatest challenge for members of the family of origin.

Transparent

SECTION FIVE

To Spread Our Wings

Transparent

"One can never consent to creep when one feels the impulse to soar" — *Helen Keller*

The final segment is devoted to moving forward. Regrettably, my view of the future is leavened by some despair, for I see, that at a policy level, we have learned little from the experiment that is adoption. To finish on a positive note, the last full essay in **To Spread Our Wings** *summarises the benefits of being open and honest with oneself and displaying generosity towards the other members of the family of origin. I acknowledge the importance of the birth mother, the adult child **and** the birth father. I also reinforce the criticality of dialogue among the persons separated from one another by an adoption. I eschew pretence, artifice and hiding the truth.*

The title of the following essay is not mis-spelt. However, it is inspired by an error in the recorded name of a presentation to the 8th Australian Conference on Adoption, held in Adelaide, South Australia in April 2004. The heading of the keynote address should have appeared both in the Conference Program and projected on a screen behind the speaker as Whither Adoption? *The careless proof-reading that let the missing 'h' escape notice has created the perfect heading under which I can have my say about the future of adoption.*

1. Wither adoption

When I toured New Zealand in 2004, I was dismayed to hear the view that contemporary 'open' adoptions are better than the 'closed' adoptions of the past. This assertion was based on the claim that, because the birth parents and their child within an adoptive family maintain contact, the issues arising from the original separation are diminished. It is as if "having an open adoption removes the pain" (Blau, 1993, p43). I believe that this judgment is foolhardy, because, taking an adopted person's viewpoint, many involved in open adoptions have yet to reach adulthood. In the case of Australia, open adoptions have been "an element of adoption practice for around fifteen years" (Fitzhardinge, 2005, p9). Accordingly, it is difficult to reach a broad conclusion about the outcomes of this arrangement. What is known is that open adoptions, unenforceable legally, sometimes break down in the early years. Communication ceases and, in essence, the adoption becomes closed. Those who 'close' open adoptions, without consulting the other parties involved, act selfishly. When an open adoption is terminated by the adoptive parents, birth parents may feel betrayed and devastated; they have lost their child not once, but twice. I do not consider open adoptions to be an advance on closed adoptions, because the child is still raised by parents who are not the original mother and father.

An adoption, once legalised, is final. It cannot be rescinded, for it consigns a child to be forever the member of an adoptive family, which she joins as a stranger. Furthermore, on a legal basis, it severs the bond between birth parents and their child and in its place, through the issuing of a replacement birth certificate, creates the falsehood that the child belongs within the adoptive family. The birth parents are assigned a new role. They are unknown persons associated with the past. To put it another way, an adoption debases a natural kinship, creating in its place an artificial relationship with people who are not known to the child.

Where an adoption crosses racial and cultural borders, the adopted child is obviously different, accentuating that the newcomer is from another place. Whilst it might be argued that this situation promotes open discussion about the child's origins, the legacy for the child may be an acute awareness of not belonging within the adoptive family. If the birth parents are unknown because of poor record-keeping in the child's country of origin or the adoptive parents use distance to discourage contact between the adopted person and his birth parents on another continent, then the adopted person may suffer an identity crisis.

Addressing the issue of identity, Western Australia, in 2003, made amendments to the state's Adoption Act, which legislated the right for a child to retain his or her first name. The provision acknowledges that the child already has a first name given by the birth parent(s) and that this name ought to be respected. If adoptive parents wish to change the child's given name, then they must demonstrate that there are special circumstances to do so. Jennifer Newbould wrote of this enshrinement: "Adoption is based on loss. However, the loss of a name is an unnecessary loss ... To honour threads that strengthen the sense of continuity of their life, rather than severance, can only assist [an adopted person to develop] a secure identity" (2004, p5).

In a 2004 Supreme Court ruling, Justice John Bryson warned that under the recently proclaimed New South Wales Adoption Act adoptive parents no longer had an unrestricted right to change the name given their child by the birth parents. He pointed out that because children adopted from overseas are removed from everything that is familiar, retaining their original name contributed to their sense of identity and somewhat ameliorated the physical and cultural dislocation embodied by an intercountry adoption.

Canadian author Isabel Huggan, in her memoir *Belonging*, about the meaning of 'home', describes meeting a young Vietnamese woman at the airport in Paris. Maguy is waiting for her French adoptive mother to collect her. "She has just been to visit the nuns in Hue [at the orphanage where she was kept until adopted, aged three], wanting to see if she could find her real mother, her real father, her family. Her self. But even though she gets some information and discovers part of her history, in the long run, she says, she is no further ahead. 'I do not know who I am or what I am ... I feel like nothing' " (2004, p122).

Howarth observes that "adoption should not be dressed up in terms of simply providing 'unwanted babies' for people who are kind and generous enough to welcome an unknown child into their home. It should be defined in terms of providing the best possible environment for a child whose [birth] parents, for whatever reason, are unable to do so. And it must also be remembered that no person, no matter what age or legal status, can be owned by another" (1988, p188). On the specific subject of intercountry adoption, Howarth concludes that if prospective "adoptive parents really have the best interests of 'unwanted' or 'abandoned' children at heart, the thousands upon thousands of dollars they spend in virtually 'buying' children to grace their own homes would have far more value and help a far greater number of children if it were put to use in preventing the circumstances in which children are relinquished for adoption" (1988, p194).

In the wake of the tsunamis that hit south Asia and east Africa in December 2004, many American citizens asked their Department of State whether it would be possible to adopt children who had been orphaned by the disaster. The Department replied on their website: "Staying with relatives in extended family units is recognized as a generally better solution than uprooting the children completely." They suggested that making financial contributions to the relief effort would provide immediate, effective assistance for these children. I applaud this stance, which, although Howarth was not contemplating such a catastrophe when she offered her views in 1988, reinforces her position.

Intercountry adoption is seen by some as a solution to decreasing fertility in the western world and over-population in the developing countries. Some countries, for example Italy, pride themselves on their humanitarian stance and deride others for impeding intercountry adoption. Paradoxically, those countries with the greatest population growth, for example in Africa, are often the least favoured sources of adopted persons.

There is evidence that within some developed countries of the world, adoption is still viewed, not from the point of view of the best interests of the child, but the needs of the prospective adoptive parents. Adoption agencies assist potential adoptive parents to find the child they want locally, or elsewhere within the country. In 2002, whilst waiting to give blood, I was drawn to the cover of *Marie Claire* magazine, on which the word 'adoption' appeared. Inside, I found an article called *Adoptees on Parade*. It described foster children in the United States of America, aged between three and sixteen, who promenaded before an audience of prospective adoptive parents in a large shopping centre. The event had been well publicised, profiles of the children were handed out and each was dressed in their best clothes. On the occasion reported, fifteen of the 36 children were selected for adoption. The prospective adoptive parents spoken to extolled the selection process – it was so much more personal than choosing children over the Internet. One girl said that her greatest fear was that she would be found to be not good enough by her adoptive family and so sent back to join the parade. Some of the children confronted the trauma of potential rejection by pretending that the event was a fashion show; others resented it for being a 'meat market'. I maintain that this is appalling treatment of children. Further, in my opinion, the prospective adoptive parents who took part should automatically be excluded from being considered fit to raise someone else's child. They are not persons equipped to take on the responsibility of raising children born to other parents.

Frisch reports another disturbing event in the United States. In certain stores, baby dolls are displayed to "look enticing to little girls. The babies are described as 'anxiously awaiting a loving home'. A prospective adopter is encouraged to choose a doll that looks like her and to reject a doll that does not meet her idea of perfection. She fills out an application form, which is quickly approved ... The adopter receives a falsified birth certificate on which is written the baby name she chose, a falsified date of birth (the date of adoption may be used), and her own name as having given birth" (2004a, p3). As Frisch goes on to point out, "the adoption industry has become increasingly clever in shaping public opinion in order to obtain babies and build a market for them. Getting little girls involved through play-acted infant adoption ... may be the best method yet." She concludes: "Teaching children that babies are more special if purchased by you rather than born to you should ensure the adoption industry [has] a market for babies well into the future" (*ibid*). In the same article, Frisch asserts that adoption lawyers cannot be expected to be honest with the birth parents, when their monetary interests lie with meeting the needs of adoptive parents. Nor are 'adoption professionals' likely to provide information about the impact of separation on birth parent and child, when their task is to find (and be rewarded for) healthy infants to place with adopting families.

I am horrified by this practice of buying children and treating them as chattels. I also abhor the reinforcement of the myth of the chosen child and the passing of falsehoods from one generation to another.

That adoption meets the needs of the child is a common refrain. Because an infant cannot articulate his needs, what is in the best interests of the child is, of necessity, an adult projection. How then, can adults remove children from their families of origin and place them instead with families who are strangers, especially when research indicates that an infant's basic needs of safety and security are undermined by the initial separation? How can adults deliberately erase a child's name, an important link to his identity, instead providing him with given and surnames that perpetuate the lie that the infant was born to his adoptive parents? These are hardly the actions of sensitive, caring adults.

It might be argued that placing a child with adoptive parents meets the child's basic physiological needs, those of shelter and sustenance. However, the evidence suggests that a human's other needs, such as a sense of belonging, feeling good about oneself and self-actualisation can be eroded by the practice called adoption.

The separation of child and birth parents creates a wound, represented by the various manifestations of grief, such as anger, guilt, shame, numbness, confusion, helplessness and sorrow, which can impede the achievement of the full development of human potential. This does not imply necessarily that those who experience an adoption are consigned forever to a lesser life, but it does mean that if they are to achieve lasting contentment, they are faced with the task of acknowledging the impact of their adoption experience and integrating the results into their lives.

During the child's upbringing, an inclusive, sensitive adoptive family environment, one that acknowledges the original heritage and present psychological needs can promote a healthy adjustment for the adopted person. These are some of the challenges that adopted persons and adoptive parents confront, ones that are often absent, unless disfunctionality is a factor, for families of origin that remain intact.

In the case of intercountry adopted persons, there are, in my view, additional hurdles to overcome. A person adopted from overseas is often separated from their cultural, ethnic and racial roots. Because they are obviously not of the adoptive family, their integration may be severely compromised. Lifton notes that overseas-born adopted persons, in common with those born locally, experience the "pain and confusion about their identity", but "that they have an extra handicap in trying to form a cohesive sense of self. They have lost not only their mother but their motherland and their mother tongue" (1994, p78). Ormerod points out that a contemporary Swedish study concluded that intercountry adopted persons are many times more likely than Swedish-born children to commit suicide, be involved in drug abuse or commit criminal acts (2004, p6).

I maintain that historically it has been rare for adoption agencies, social workers and prospective adoptive parents to have taken the consequences of adoption into account when they have considered the placement of a child. Today, this is why the benign face of adoption, as presented in the popular press, is so irresponsible, for it perpetuates the myth that separating children from parents who were not in a position to care for them brings relief to the birth mother and provides the child with a family, blessed by the attention of two loving parents, who raise the child as if she had been born to them ... happily ever after. The truth about the consequences of adoption needs to be conveyed, by practitioners and an accountable media alike, not only to destroy the falsehoods, but to give those affected by adoption an uncensored voice. Because the conventional view amongst the public, the majority of whom have not experienced the impact of adoption first hand, is that adoption is a panacea, it can be difficult for those with adoption experiences to challenge the norm. Utterances of the truth may be viewed as whining and weakness, rather than what they are – awareness and strength.

Time and time again, when I attend support group meetings, I am struck by the rawness of the pain that adopted persons and birth parents display. However, when I place the actual representation into context, I realise that these people are the fortunate few. The people who show a willingness to articulate their story and their feelings are but a fraction of those with adoption experiences, even within a city of the size of Melbourne. (Given that, since 1968 there have been approximately 20,000 local non-relative adoptions in Victoria, with an adopted person and two birth parents for each adoption, against a background of the population of Melbourne constituting about 60% of the state's total, 36,000 people represents a substantial number of metropolitan residents with direct family of origin experiences.)

Sadly, there are those affected by adoption who are unwilling to acknowledge the truth that their adoption experience is painful, for reasons that lie within themselves. Their reluctance to be open is perhaps reinforced by a social expectation that they should accept their lot and get on with life. These, the unfortunate many, are the people whose abilities to live a full and authentic life are compromised.

I have heard some birth parents and some adopted people say that they do not think about their past; they prefer to live in the present. I maintain that these people not only miss out on understanding facets of who they are, but they also deny themselves the opportunity to consider the other members of their birth family.

Of course, if the members of families of origin were not separated in the first instance, then the consequences of an adoption would not be a discussion point. If energies were to be devoted to preserving families rather than destroying them, then the interests of the child would, in many cases, be better served. Addressing the core issues, such as parenting skills, financial support and housing that may seem to be barriers to sustaining the family is surely a more child-focussed approach than adoption. Many birth mothers and birth fathers have said that they regret losing their child to adoption, adding that it casts a pall over their lives. It is difficult to envisage a parent ever regretting keeping his or her child. My daughter, a mother for the first time in 2003, said to me in 2004, "How can any parent ever give up a child?" She was not taking me to task for my role as a relinquishing father, but rather expressing wonderment about the primal bond that connects parent and child.

On the global stage, adoption is often a prematurely assigned permanent solution for a family that could be experiencing temporary difficulties. The circumstances that led to the decision to place a child for adoption may change. For example, the birth parents may have at the time they signed the consent forms lacked the financial resources to support their child. This does not mean that they would always be impecunious. Their impoverishment may be temporary and capable of being rectified. Alternatively, they may have lacked the support of their parents. Again, this is a factor, that with time and reconsideration, may have changed, meaning that the child could be accepted as a member of the extended families of the birth parents. I believe that, given the finality of an adoption, it is incumbent upon the parents to explore ways to overcome any barriers that may prevent the family of origin from remaining intact.

Resources, such as adoption agency social workers, have a key role to play in keeping families together. They have an obligation not only to help the couple considering adoption to investigate the means of overcoming any apparent hurdles, but also to point out the consequences of adoption for the child and each birth parent. Frisch reinforces this point when she writes: "The very people counseling [the birth mother] could acknowledge her as the mother of her child and help her keep her child. Nurses, doctors and others could disclose the known effects of separation on a mother and her child" (2004b, p11). Frisch then provides examples of the assistance that can be offered, such as direct financial support, shared housing and the availability of government programmes, all with the objective of "educating everyone in the community about the most loving option – keeping family together" (*ibid*). Instructive material about the impact of adoption on family members does exist. In New

Zealand, videos of people talking honestly about their adoption experiences are made available to adults considering adoption, *ie* the prospective birth and adoptive parents.

Stromberg makes a telling observation, when she notes in her study of North American birth fathers that there has been a recent shift in the notion of their villainy. Today, the birth father is a villain not because he disappears, but because he "comes in to contest the adoption placement and ultimately causes what has been labeled an 'adoption disruption' " (2002, p14). I contend that these men, intent on preventing an adoption and keeping a family intact, are heroes, not villains.

I maintain that adoption is a social experiment that has failed. The damage caused to families of origin by adoption is too great for the practice to be maintained. The alternative 'root cause' approach better meets the needs of families, as it is intent upon preservation rather than destruction. If keeping the family of origin together proves impossible, then, as a last resort, alternative care, preferably on a temporary basis, could be considered. If a child's name is changed, with this re-assignment goes an essence of their identity. Dual identities not only create confusion within, but they also initiate the secrets and lies which inhibit parent–child communication and create barriers to the achievement of human potential.

Further, in today's social climate, an original justification for the issuing of an adoptive birth certificate (to mask the stain of illegitimacy and so protect the few) is not as relevant as it once was, because of the overall increase in the number of children born outside marriage. In New Zealand, for example, in the first year of the twenty-first century, 44 per cent of births were to unmarried women, up from eight per cent in 1962 (Larson, 2005, p40).

Adoption deserves to wither and perish. Adopted person Jerry Stadtmiller is a person who has, using a cause and effect approach, reached the same conclusion: "There's always going to be pain in adoption, and it is insanity to consider adoption without pain, open or closed." As a result, his solution is to "outlaw adoption" (Blau, 1993, p43).

Adoption is a social experiment that belongs in the past. However, for those who have suffered the legacy of adoption, this past is very much a part of their present and their future. These people would appreciate the understanding and support of the community as they draw upon resources, within and without, to acknowledge, share and comprehend their individual adoption experiences.

The recognition and erosion of misconceptions benefits not only adopted persons and birth parents, but also those within their sphere. Such welcome candour may indeed hasten the end of adoption, equated for so long with suppression and falsehoods. May the day when we can look back on the trial called adoption and shake our heads in sorrow be near.

The final article contains suggestions that evolve from the preceding chapters. The emphasis here is on practical advice to help those affected by adoption to incorporate the experience into their lives. Only by shunning deceit, secrecy and denial and embracing, in their stead, honesty, openness and generosity to yourself and to others, are equilibrium and personal growth achievable.

2. Recommendations for living an authentic life

The following suggestions are a guide to assist those people with an adoption experience to live a rich and fulfilling life. They are based on my observations and those of others who have written and spoken about the events that shaped their post-adoption lives.

Be open, be honest

Living with secrets and denial is living a lie. By embracing these barriers to truth, you are consigning yourself to a partial life, one beset by angst and distrust. Preserving secrets is energy-sapping. Efforts devoted to withholding information about the past undermine one's capacity to live in the present and to anticipate a promising future. The energy devoted to self-deceit and suppression is negative, with the likely consequence of inertia. Likewise, bitterness about and blaming others for your adoption experience prevents personal progress.

There is a remedy for an unfulfilling existence – to disown the inhibitors and install in their place the growth generators of honesty, openness and generosity. Confronting the unpalatable may seem risky, but I can guarantee that when you do take action, you will feel unburdened, more positive in your outlook and more welcoming of and appreciated by others. Dealing with the past is absolutely a risk worth taking. In my opinion, admitting to the denial you have practised to protect yourself is the first necessary step to personal healing. In doing so you may expose the secret about your past, which you have deliberately withheld from others, not because of the content of your revelations, but rather what you believed they might think of you. I know that the admission to myself that I had wronged two people decades previously was a breakthrough, the one that I needed to make before I could begin work on revealing my adoption experience. Fundamentally, recovery is not possible for the person who is intent on preserving secrets, whether this be self-deceit and/or deliberately withholding information from others. Anger, used productively, rather than with bitterness to effect change, may assist self-enlightenment and provide guidance or inspiration for others. The application of positive energy and personal responsibility are essential, if you aim to live a rewarding life.

Acknowledge your experience

Be aware that, as a participant, an adoption creates a chain of cause and effect responses. Recognise that as the result of being adopted or losing a child to adoption, the way you feel about yourself may have suffered. Accept that adoption represents loss and that loss results in grief – for all members of the family of origin. If you acknowledge that grief is what you experience when the family of origin is split, then you are in a position to address the accompanying feelings of profound sorrow, anger, shame and guilt, as well as the various fears, such as rejection, intimacy and being controlled by circumstances and other people.

Grief need not be a debilitator; it can be incorporated into your life. You can learn from the mourning protocols that accompany other bereavements. *Adoption and Recovery: Solving the mystery of reunion*, by Evelyn Robinson is an excellent resource, not only to understand the grief resulting from an adoption loss, but to develop the personal strategies to mend. Processing grief, through self-awareness and taking personal responsibility, is the path to self-acceptance and healing.

Share and assimilate

I believe that sharing your adoption experience not only with yourself but also with others is therapeutic. In my case, I have chosen to listen and to write, in order to achieve understanding. As a result, I have come to know myself better. I now comprehend the impact my life-changing decisions had on myself and on the two people my actions affected directly, Kay and our son James.

Some people may choose to share their story orally. It is essential that you seek a non-judgmental setting to deliver your revelations. Support groups are often a good starting point. I recommend, rather than joining a mixed support group, comprising birth parents, adopted persons and adoptive parents, that at first you associate with a smaller group, one which represents your affiliation. Here, as you begin your release, you are likely to feel more at ease with those who share your perspective, whether, for example, it be birth mothers who have lost children to adoption, or adopted persons who have grown up away from their family of origin. When you feel that you are ready to explore further, you may consider joining a broader group to listen to the views from the other side of the separation divide. In this setting you are also well placed to offer your perspective, to assist their understanding of what it means to you to be parted from the members of your birth family. (For birth fathers, this ideal sequence may not be possible. There may be insufficient fathers to form a dedicated support group. An alternative for these men may be to form an on-line chat group, before moving on to join a local mixed support group.)

Other ways of opening up can be via music, painting, drawing or sculpture and perhaps even comedy. If you find that your explorations are driven by a rage founded on blame and bitterness, I suggest that you seek professional help from an expert. Some psychologists and counsellors have little or no understanding of the grief that accompanies adoption, so make sure that you ask some background questions before you choose and begin paying.

Understand your feelings

I maintain that sharing your experience and listening to others is but an initial step on the path to healing. The freedom gained by exposing personal pain and having your feelings validated by others with similar feelings can be cathartic. However, there is more to be achieved. It is important that you give your adoption experience a realistic setting. It is helpful to determine why you feel the way you do about your adoption experience. Undermining the self-beliefs that are causing you anxiety could prove to be beneficial. Here the insights of others, whether, for example, they be authors or counsellors, can be of enormous benefit. Most post-adoption support organisations maintain excellent libraries and these are a useful resource. You may find that at first you are drawn to the personal stories of others and that their narratives provide exposure to a wide range of adoption experiences. It is likely that you will wish to seek deeper insights and this is where books that provide contexts for adoption experiences prove to be invaluable. From these you may find explanations that help you to understand why, for example, you feel sad, relationships are difficult and you seem to be controlled by events. Be careful, for some books that purport to aid understanding can prove to be misleading. The more texts you read, the more discerning you are likely to become. For me, *The Primal Wound*, by Nancy Verrier and *Adoption and Loss: The Hidden Grief*, by Evelyn Robinson, were essential to my personal growth and I would recommend these books as sound starting points.

Explore the background

Healing may benefit from a retrospective analysis of the circumstances that resulted in an adoption. For birth parents, it can be helpful to consider the family and social setting in which you were raised. Your family may not have been close-knit and therefore not in a position to offer you support upon hearing the news of unplanned motherhood or fatherhood. Community attitudes of the time perhaps conditioned the family to promote the adoption option and so protect themselves from stigmatisation. Those arranging the placement of the child may simply have reinforced plans already decreed by the extended family, albeit in many cases, without the specific say-so of the birth mother and/or the birth father.

The guilt and the shame that birth parents often heap upon themselves may, with the passing of time and an increasing awareness of the circumstances in which the adoption took place, become less burdensome. Dialogue between the birth parents and their respective parents may enhance a comprehension of the environment in which each birth parent was raised and the conditions that precipitated their being separated from their child. These discussions may unblock the past, thus allowing recovery work to proceed.

For adopted persons, who have no cognitive awareness of the events surrounding their adoption, the available avenues may be reading about and listening to the experiences of others. Social histories can assist; also the narratives of other adopted persons who have achieved reunion. The circumstances of their own adoption, as told by the birth parents, may, if reunion occurs, be the best source of information.

Be self-responsible

Many people enter reunion without adequate preparation. Some believe, falsely, that reunion will resolve their adoption issues and how they feel about themselves. These people perhaps do not understand the meaning of their adoption experience, but expect to be mended by meeting a family member from whom they were separated. This devolution of responsibility not only places unwarranted pressure on the other person, but it also creates a self-expectation that is unlikely to be met.

Only you can mend yourself. You place yourself in a position to accomplish this if you make the effort to acknowledge and process your adoption experience. You are then better placed to enter reunion and to achieve an outcome that provides a sense of accomplishment and healing for you. If you are fortunate enough to enter reunion with another member of your birth family who has also worked on their adoption issues, then the possibilities for a sustained and fulfilling relationship, are, I believe, enhanced. Do not wait for reunion to begin work on understanding what adoption means for you. If you have not already started, now is the time.

Don't neglect the birth father

Considerations of loss and grief as they impact upon families that are separated by an adoption can benefit from the inclusion of the birth father. The father is joined genetically and, if aware of his paternity, psychologically to his child. Studies by Cicchini (1993), Stromberg (2002), Clapton (2003) and Coles (2004) demonstrate that the lost child frequently remains in the thoughts of the father and that he, the male parent, suffers separation wounds.

For some fathers and mothers, there may be an additional factor. The adoption may have interrupted a significant relationship. A residual affectional bond may remain between the birth parents. Each birth parent may experience a lingering emotional attachment to the other. Whilst both birth parents perhaps believe that they lost not only a child but the other birth parent, a birth mother's response is likely to be disappointment that her relationship with the birth father, if significant at the time, ended before or at the time of the adoption. A birth father's experience may be more complex and centred on the traditional role of provider/protector, which he has failed to fulfil for his partner. His regrets at the severing of the relationship may be compounded by guilt for having failed to stand by the birth mother and, by association, the child she was carrying or had recently given birth to. A birth father may feel that he is responsible for changing the lives of two people, the mother and her child, whereas a mother's remorse typically centres on the socially expected nurturing role she has been unable to perform for her infant.

A dual focus, reinforced by guilt, may affect the pattern of a birth father's search. He may wish to contact the birth mother first to resolve outstanding issues with her, before he moves on to search for his adult child. However, some fathers may be so confused about whom to seek first that they do nothing, opting instead to be the subject of a search. If he waits to be found and he is unsought, the father runs the risk of not meeting the other members of his birth family.

As Coles (2004) and Pace (2004a) in particular have demonstrated, rapprochement between the birth parents can promote healing for the birth mother and the birth father. This in turn may have a ripple effect on the quality of the reunions between the individual birth parents and their adult child.

For adopted persons and birth mothers, as well as professional persons such as counsellors and social workers, I suggest that acknowledgment and tolerance be accorded birth fathers. It may prove useful to contemplate the possibility that the man who appeared to be mean-spirited at the time of the birth and the adoption has, with the passage of time and maturity, become remorseful and troubled about his part in those long ago events.

Stay positive in the face of setbacks

If you reach out, seeking reunion with the person from whom you were separated at the time of the adoption and you receive a rebuff, try not to take it personally. It is likely that the person whom you have contacted has not rejected you. Rather it is probable that they have not yet faced their adoption issues, so as to be in a position where they feel ready to join you in reunion. The rebuff may seem harsh and permanent, but I suggest that you do not try to guess the reasons why your offer has been declined. You might consider how it was for you when you felt uncomfortable, perhaps even petrified about facing your adoption issues. Strive to be patient and exercise consideration. You can draw comfort from the fact that the other member of your family of origin is aware that you care about them.

Approaching a parent–child reunion from the perspective of what you can offer, rather than what you want is beneficial for both parties. For a birth parent, presenting opportunities for the other to know you, to be available to answer questions about the circumstances of the adoption and any other matters, such as heritage and well-being, displays humanity. I believe that it is not threatening if you occasionally remind the person with whom you seek reunion that you continue to care about them. A birthday and Christmas can be the appropriate times to send your best wishes. I suggest that you keep your written messages short, simple and unemotional. Because you send a card does not mean that you should anticipate one in return, either thanking you, or for your birthday or at Christmas time. I have sent cards to my son now for several years; not once have they been acknowledged, yet I feel that they have a place in his life. A useful way to consider your reaching out twice a year is to view it as an opportunity to issue the other person with a subtle invitation to participate in reunion. You are, without saying as much, keeping the possibility of a reunion open, by conveying your wishes in a caring, non-threatening manner. I believe that there would be few recipients who would object to the spirit of the messages. Another possible benefit for the recipient is that they may feel reassured that you, the sender, were not offended by their decline of your original offer. Further, through his 'no-obligation' approach, the initiator of the regular communication appears to be prepared to give you, the recipient, space and wait until **you** are ready for reunion.

Bear in mind, however, that nobody is immortal. In the situation where the recipient of the cards is the adopted person, birth parents, like everybody else, have a finite life and they may have expired of old age (and worn out their patience!) before their 'child' is ready to sanction reunion.

A message for birth fathers

I encourage more birth fathers to own up to their adoption experiences. Considering what I have learned about myself and what I have heard from a regrettably small sample of birth fathers, I maintain that admitting to and addressing the past is therapeutic.

Just as the father played a seminal role in the events that precipitated the adoption, so too does he have a vital part to play in addressing the legacy of the family of origin being split. On this basis, I contend that a birth father's recovery must include consideration of both the birth mother and the child. Personal recovery is important, but a mark of a birth father's generosity is to embrace the other members of the family of origin. In my opinion, seeking information about the mother and the child does not, in isolation, display charity; it meets personal needs only. Further, those birth fathers who do nothing at all about acknowledging and addressing their adoption issues are consigned to remaining stuck in denial. Birth fathers who obtain information and then proceed no further, are in my view, still cocooned and averse to taking risks.

As with other members of the separated family, to progress a birth father must be adventurous and prepared to reach out. For him, this involves contacting and seeking reunion with the adult adopted person, as well as the birth mother. A birth father must be prepared to give of himself to assist their mending – the birth mother and the adult adopted person can choose whether or not to avail themselves of the opportunity that he is offering. A birth father's willingness to help applies not only to his taking the initiative, but also the tone and content of his response to an outreach made by his adult child or the birth mother.

Anecdotally, it seems that many birth fathers remain timid, afraid of the consequences of communicating with the other members of the family of origin. My view is that it is better to try and to know, than not to have tried at all.

I concede that there are birth fathers who are not aware that they have fathered a child who was subsequently adopted. Also, I recognise that some jurisdictions have in the past disallowed or discouraged the entry of the birth father's name on the birth record. This oversight, in situations where the birth father knows his status, he may, legally, be in a position to correct. However, it seems that few men choose to acknowledge their paternity retrospectively. These matters may explain, in the case of New Zealand (where statistics are available), the discrepancy between applications made by birth mothers and birth fathers for identifying information about their adopted children. Overall, for the period from 1986 to date, applications by birth mothers outstrip applications by birth fathers by a factor of almost 8:1. In the first years of the twenty-first century (a subset), the ratio is close to 4:1, but the number of applications per annum by birth fathers has barely shifted. (Note, these statistics relate only to requests for information – no statistics are kept on what the requesters do with the information and whether it is used to make contact. The number of reunions that result is unknown.) On a 2004 tour of New Zealand, I did not see either the overall ratio or the recent ratio replicated at adoption seminars; rather the ratio of birth mothers to birth fathers was more like 25:1.

Sadly, birth fathers are present in small numbers at public forums about post-adoption matters and, I suspect, as initiators of reunion. Only birth fathers can alter this imbalance. I urge them to do so, otherwise the voice of the birth father will remain subdued and the stereotype of the callous, invisible man preserved, to the detriment of all affected by adoption. Birth fathers have too much to offer to themselves, the other members of the family of origin and the community, to remain in the background.

Be inclusive, be generous

During the grieving and the healing phases, I believe that all members of the family of origin warrant consideration. An adoption coincided with the disintegration of a family; these same three family members display awareness and responsibility if they ensure that they integrate their adoption experiences into their lives. Each also has the opportunity to demonstrate generosity, by assisting the other family members with their recoveries. Mother, father and adult child all benefit if they each display a willingness to be equal participants in interpersonal recovery work. The three dyads of mother and child, father and child and the two parents were separated by the adoption. To promote personal integration, I recommend that the same pairings seek reunion, from which interpersonal reconciliations may result. If the complete triad of birth mother, birth father and adopted person do not involve themselves in search and reunion, then, in my view, personal and interpersonal healing for each is, by definition, compromised.

Recover your self and live

For healing to occur, the will to advance, transparency and persistence are essential. Based on personal experience and information supplied by others, I maintain that people with adoption experiences cannot move forward until they have dealt with the barriers and the inhibitors associated with the past.

I am convinced that it is impossible for persons with adoption experiences to live authentic lives unless and until they have acknowledged their losses, processed the accompanying grief and incorporated the effects of the original parent–child separation into their lives. (For birth parents, there is also the severance of their relationship to consider.) Grieving the loss caused by an adoption is healthy and productive. To address the grief displays awareness, personal responsibility and commitments to openness, honesty and growth. Your generosity embraces the people you care about, including yourself – a potent, positive legacy for all directly affected by the original adoption. Letting go of any blame or resentment and forgiving yourself and others encompassed by your adoption narrative confirms your generosity. For those who are not ready to reconsider their position, I urge patience. Given time, they may be influenced by your generosity.

Ignoring the loss, grief and other consequences may have a negative compounding effect, which is likely to inhibit personal growth. In my view, pretending that the adoption has had no impact on your life is not a feasible alternative, unless you wish to condemn yourself to a constrained existence. To accept this latter scenario mutely is to waste the opportunity for a life celebrated.

Figure 2 summarises the personal management of the impact of adoption. Participants have a clear choice between letting the growth inhibitors of deceit, secrecy and denial hold sway or embracing the growth generators of honesty, openness and generosity. The diagram highlights the consequences of being beholden to restraining self-beliefs. More importantly, it displays the personal benefits of opting to be proactive; of creating a new paradigm.

Figure 2: **Post-adoption Hurting and Healing – A Summary**					
Anxieties (based on self-beliefs) **+**	**Growth Inhibitors**	**...**	**Commitments** (driven by self-determination) **+**	**Growth Generators**
Guilt – caused adoption to occur			Acknowledge the impact of the adoption on you	
Shame – deserve misfortune	*Deceit*			*Honesty*
Disempowerment – emotional turmoil occurs when not in control of own destiny	*Secrecy*		Take personal responsibility for addressing the pain	
Rejection – come to expect, because of personal deficiencies			Explore and understand your reactions to loss and grief	*Openness*
Intimacy – getting close may re-enact original loss	*Denial*		Mend, both by delving in and reaching out	*Generosity*
⇓	⇓		⇓	⇓
Consequences			**Results**	
• Self-protection • Interpersonal inertia • Stuck in the past • Fragmented, static existence			• Self-discovery (personal recovery and well-being) • Interpersonal recovery (reunion) • Live in the present; welcome the future • Integrated, fulfilling life	

A personal validation

Today I reflect – my worst and my best decisions, those which have had the greatest influence on the way I feel about my adult life, are related to the same event, albeit separated by a gap of a quarter of a century. I chose to be absent when my son was born and adopted; my life changed for the better when I decided to deal with the consequences of my earlier neglect. Based on my experience, I contend that when you make the effort to address the loss and the grief caused when a family is separated by an adoption, you will feel much better about yourself. I know for certain which of the two phases of my life beyond age twenty has been the more satisfying.

Heed basic truths

For me, the benefits of interpersonal and personal awareness are neatly summed up by Lao Tsu, in the classic *Tao Te Ching*:

> ***Knowing others is wisdom;***
> ***Knowing the self is enlightenment.***

3. Finally, a musing

I happened to discover the following trio of words in a book about anagrams. It struck me that, in an adoption setting, they apply uniquely to men who have been separated from their children. The words, relevant to the timing of a birth father's definite involvement, his possible feelings and the relinquished role are:

- prenatal
- paternal and
- parental

It is apt that this final observation from a birth father is about birth fathers.

References

Anderson, Carole J. *Thoughts to Consider for Newly Searching Adoptees*, Concerned United Birthparents, Inc, USA, 1997

ARCS. 'Insights', Vol 17, No 2, Winter 2004, p4 and p11

Bennett, William J. *The Book of Virtues: A Treasury of Great Moral Stories*, Simon & Schuster, USA, 1993

Blau, Eric. *Stories of Adoption: Loss and Reunion*, NewSage Press, USA, 1993

Brodzinsky, David M, Schechter, Marshall D and Henig, Robin Marantz. *Being Adopted: The Lifelong Search for Self*, Random House, USA, 1993

Brodzinsky, David. *Attachment Issues in the School-Age Adopted Child*, 'issues', Number 20, July–Sept, 2001, pp20–24

Butler-Bowdon, Tom. *50 Self-Help Classics*, Simon & Schuster (Australia) Pty Limited, Australia, 2001 [Quoted passages are from the summary of *An Intimate History of Humanity* by Theodore Zeldin]

Cameron, Fiona and West, Jane. *The Impacts of Shame – Secrecy and Denial on the Adoption Process*, Abstracts of 8th Australian Conference on Adoption, Adelaide, April 2004, pp56–57

Carlini, Heather. *Adoptee Trauma: A Counselling Guide For Adoptees*, Morning Side Publishing, Canada, 1993

Cicchini, Mercurio. *Development of Responsibility: The Experience of Birth Fathers in Adoption*, Adoption Research & Counselling Service, Inc, Australia, 1993

Clapton, Gary. *Birth Fathers and their Adoption Experiences*, Jessica Kingsley Publishers, United Kingdom, 2003

Coles, Gary. *Being a Birthfather*, 'Proceedings of "Adoption Looking Forward Looking Back" Conference', Canterbury Adoption Awareness and Education Trust, New Zealand, 1998, pp119–120

Coles, Gary. *Understanding Birth Fathers*, VANISH Incorporated, Australia, 2002

Coles, Gary. *Ever After: Fathers and the Impact of Adoption*, Clova Publications, Australia, 2004

Coon, Dennis. *Introduction to Psychology: Exploration and Application (Sixth Edition)*, West Publishing Company, USA, 1992

Cordray, Bill. *Reproductive Technologies: Emotional Adoption*, 'Decree', American Adoption Congress, Spring/Summer 2000, pp11–12

Dent, Mark. *A good day to walk: My encounter with bone cancer*, David Lovell Publishing, Australia, 1997

Doka, Kenneth. *Disenfranchised Grief: Recognising Hidden Sorrow*, Lexington Books, USA, 1989

Ferguson, Stephen. *Coming Full* Circle, A presentation at seminars organised by VANISH and AFRS, Melbourne, Australia, July 2005

Fisher, Florence. *The Search for Anna Fisher*, Michael Dempsey, United Kingdom, 1973

Fitzhardinge, Helen. *Open Adoption in Practice*, 'Branching Out', Volume 12, Number 1, March 2005, pp9–10

Frisch, Laurie. *Saks Newborn Nursery® Infant Adoption: What is the Message to Little Girls?*, 'CUB Communicator', Summer/Fall 2004a, p3

Frisch, Laurie. *Dear Birthmother – Is Adoption Worth the Grief?*, 'CUB Communicator', Summer/Fall 2004b, p5 and p11

Gediman, Judith and Brown, Linda. *BirthBond: Reunions Between Birthparents and Adoptees – What Happens After...*, New Horizon Press, USA, 1991

Gillard-Glass, Sheryn and England, Jan. *Adoption New Zealand: The never-ending story*, HarperCollinsPublishers, New Zealand, 2002

Griffith, Keith. *The Right To Know Who You Are: Reform of Adoption Law with Honesty, Openness and Integrity*, Katherine W Kimbell, Canada, 1991

Harkness, Libby. *Looking for Lisa*, Random House, Australia, 1991

Harrison, Michael. *Do You Dare?*, in Calwell, Sue and Johnson, Daniel, *There's More to Life than Sex & Money: 103 inspirational stories to give your life new meaning*, Penguin Books, Australia, 1997, pp69–70

Hartman, Ann. *Secrecy in Adoption*, in Evan Imber-Black, *Secrets in Families and Family Therapy*, WW Norton & Company, USA, 1993, pp86–105

Hendrix, Harville. *Keeping the Love You Find: A Personal Guide*, Pocket Books, USA, 1992

Hochman, Gloria, Huston, Anna and Prowler, Mady. *Issues facing Adult Adoptees*, 'issues', Number 12, Oct–Dec 1998, pp11–12

Howard, Sally. *Finding me in a paper bag: Searching for both sides now*, Gateway Press, Inc, USA, 2003

Howarth, Ann. *Reunion*, Penguin Books, New Zealand, 1988

Huggan, Isabel. *Belonging*, Bantam, Australia, 2004

Imber-Black, Evan. *An Overview*, in Evan Imber-Black, *Secrets in Families and Family Therapy*, WW Norton & Company, USA, 1993, pp18–27

Iwanek, Mary. *Debunking myths and building bridges: the reality of adoption*, 'Social Work Now', Number 9, April 1998, pp25–30

Jones, Mary Bloch. *Birthmothers: Women who have relinquished babies for adoption tell their stories*, Chicago Review Press, USA, 1993

Kaplan, Sharon and Silverstein, Deborah. *Seven Core Issues in Adoption*, in Keith Griffith, *The Right To Know Who You Are: Reform of Adoption Law with Honesty, Openness and Integrity*, Katherine W Kimbell, Canada, 1991, Section 2, pp1–4

Kirk, H David. *Shared Fate: A Theory and Method of Adoptive Relationships,* [Revised edition], Ben-Simon Publications, USA, 1984

Krestan, Jo-Ann and Bepko, Claudia. *On Lies, Secrets and Silence: The Multiple Levels of Denial in Addictive Families*, in Evan Imber-Black, *Secrets in Families and Family Therapy*, WW Norton & Company, USA, 1993, pp141–159

Larson, Virginia. *The End of Family Life – As We Knew It*, 'North & South', April 2005, pp36–48

Lifton, Betty Jean. *Lost and Found: The Adoption Experience*, Harper & Row, USA, 1988 [NB: First published by Dial Press in 1979]

Lifton, Betty Jean. *Journey of the Adopted Self: A Quest for Wholeness*, Basic Books, USA, 1994

Lifton, Betty Jean. *The Adoptee's Journey*, 'Journal of Social Distress and the Homeless', Vol 11, No.2, April 2002, pp207–213

Lorbach, Caroline. *Experiences of Donor Conception: Parents, Offspring and Donors through the Years*, Jessica Kingsley Publishers, UK, 2003

Lowe, Heather. *What you should know if you're considering adoption for your baby*, Concerned United Birthparents, Inc, USA, undated

MacKay, Linda. *Creating a separate identity: differentiation and the experience of adoption*, 'issues', Number 32, Dec 2004–Feb 2005, pp12–19

Marshall, Audrey and McDonald, Margaret. *The Many-Sided Triangle: Adoption in Australia*, Melbourne University Press, Australia, 2001

Marshall, Dianne. *Would you Recognise the Loss and Grief of Adoption?*, 'issues', Number 14, April–July 1999, pp1–8

Mason, Marilyn J. *Shame: Reservoir for Family* Secrets, in Evan Imber-Black, *Secrets in Families and Family Therapy*, WW Norton & Company, USA, 1993, pp29–43

Mason, Mary Martin. *Out of the Shadows: Birthfathers' Stories*, OJ Howard Publishing, USA, 1995

Millar, Maggie. *The Right to Know: Secrecy and 'donor' conception*, 'Australian Rationalist', Number 53, Autumn 2001, pp20–24

Murray, Mary. *My Journey of Reunion: A Work in Progress*, 'ARMS Victoria Newsletter', Autumn 2002

Newbould, Jennifer. *What's in a name?*, 'Insights', Summer 2003–04, p5

New Zealand Law Commission. *Report 65: Adoption and Its Alternatives: A Different Approach and a New Framework*, New Zealand, 2000

Nicholls, Rosemary and Levy, Mina. *Relinquishment Counselling of Birth Fathers*, Chapter 6 of *The Search for Self*, ed Phillip and Shurlee Swain, The Federation Press, Australia, 1992

NSW Committee on Adoption and Permanent Care. *Further Down the Track*, Australia, 2001

Ormerod, Thea. *The Service Needs of Transracial Adoptive* Families, 'Branching Out', Volume 11, Number 2, July 2004, pp6–7

Pace, Sandra Falconer. *Review of "Ever After: Fathers and the Impact of Adoption"* on the website of the 'Canadian Council of Natural Mothers', 2004a

Pace, Sandra Falconer. *Shame*, on the website of the 'Canadian Council of Natural Mothers', 2004b

PARC. 'Branching Out', Volume 11, Number 3, October 2004

Partridge, P C. *The particular challenges of being adopted*, Smith College Studies in Social Work, 61(2), 1991, pp197–208

Pavao, Joyce Maguire. *The Family of Adoption*, Beacon Press, USA, 1998

Peck, M Scott. *The Road Less Travelled*, Arrow Books, United Kingdom, 1990

Phillips, Zara. *Chasing Away the Shadows: An Adoptee's Journey to Motherhood*, Gateway Press, USA, 2004

Portuesi, Donna. *Silent Voices heard: Impact of the Birth Mother Experience Then and Now*, 'Decree', American Adoption Congress, Spring/Summer 2000, pp5–7

Robinson, Evelyn. *Some thoughts on anger*, 'ARMS South Australia Newsletter', Autumn Edition, April 2000a, pp10–11

Robinson, Evelyn. *Adoption and Loss: The Hidden Grief*, Clova Publications, Australia, 2000b

Robinson, Evelyn. *Adoption and Loss: The Hidden Grief*, unpublished presentation to ARCS, Perth, Western Australia, 2001a

Robinson, Evelyn. *Adoption and Loss: The Hidden Grief*, unpublished presentation to BirthLink, Edinburgh, Scotland, 2001b

Robinson, Evelyn. *Post-adoption grief counselling*, 'Adoption & Fostering', Volume 26 Number 2, 2002, pp57–63

Robinson, Evelyn. *Adoption and Loss: The Hidden Grief [Revised Edition]*, Clova Publications, Australia, 2003

Robinson, Evelyn. *Adoption and Recovery: Solving the mystery of reunion*, Clova Publications, Australia, 2004

Russell, Marlou. *Adoption Wisdom: A Guide to the Issues and Feelings of Adoption*, Broken Branch Productions, USA, 1996

Schooler, Jayne. *Searching for a Past: The Adopted Adult's Unique Process of Finding Identity*, Pinon Press, USA, 1995

Small, Joanne. *Working with Adoptive Families*, 'Public Welfare', Summer, 1987, pp33–41

Sorosky, Arthur D, Baran, Annette and Pannor, Reuben. *The Adoption Triangle*, Corona Publishing Co, USA, 1989 [NB: Originally published by Anchor Press/Doubleday in 1978]

Stallings, Roger. *Birthfathers and Miracles*, 'issues', Number 31, Sept–Nov 2004, pp13–14

Steer, Isabella. *Melissa*, Newsletter of the Association of Relinquishing Mothers (Vic) Inc., Spring 2004

Stromberg, Michelle Denise. *Birth fathers and the Adoption Experience: A Narrative Exploration of the Birth Father Perspective on Adoption*, A Thesis Submitted to the Faculty of Graduate Studies and Research in Partial Fulfillment of the Requirements for the Degree of Master of Social Work, University of Regina, Canada, 2002

Taylor, Patricia. *Shadow Train*, Gateway Press, Inc, USA, 1995

Trollope, Joanna. *Brother & Sister*, Bloomsbury Publishing Plc, UK, 2004

VANISH Incorporated. 'VOICE', Winter Edition, May 2004a

VANISH Incorporated. 'VOICE', Spring Edition, September 2004b

Van Keppel, Margaret, Midford, Suzanne and Cicchini, Mercurio. *The Experience of Loss in Adoption*, paper presented at the Fifth Biennial National Conference of the National Association for Loss and Grief, Australia, 1987

Verrier, Nancy Newton. *The Primal Wound: Understanding the Adopted Child*, Gateway Press, Inc, USA, 1993

Verrier, Nancy Newton. *Coming Home to Self*, Gateway Press, Inc, USA, 2003

Wallace, John. *Between Scylla and Charybdis: Issues in alcoholism therapy*, 'Alcohol Health and Research World', Summer issue, 1977

Wegar, Kathleen. *Adoption, identity, and kinship: the debate over sealed birth records*, Yale University Press, USA, 1997

Winkler, Robin and van Keppel, Margaret. *Relinquishing Mothers in Adoption: Their Long-term Adjustment*, Melbourne Institute of Family Studies, Monograph No. 3, Australia, 1984

Witney, Celia. *The experiences of unmarried fathers whose children were surrendered for adoption: some conclusions and comments*, NPN Newsletter No 33, April 2003, p12